THE
GAME
WITHIN

INSIDE THE MINDS
OF THE
TOP GOLFING PROS

MAGAZINE

The
GAME
Within

INSIDE THE MINDS
OF THE
TOP GOLFING PROS

First published in 2003

A catalogue record for this book is available from the British Library

ISBN 1 84425 142 X

Published jointly by
Haynes Publishing, Sparkford,
Yeovil, Somerset BA22 7JJ, England
Phone 01963 440635, www.haynes.co.uk
and
Emap Active Limited,
Wentworth House, Wentworth Street,
Peterborough PE1 1DS, England
Phone 01733 213700, www.emap.com

Printed and bound in England by J.H. Haynes & Co. Ltd, Sparkford

CONTENTS

Foreword by
David Clarke

The greatest golfers in the world make fascinating studies of humanity - some have lived a lifetime in the spotlight, others are just discovering what it's like to be a superstar - legend or legend in the making, Golf World has the inside track.

In this Golfing Greats celebration of the talent and wisdom of today's elite Golf World gets under the skins of what really makes a champion, how these giants of the game are so very special, and what makes them different to we mere mortals.

Naturally Tiger Woods, the world's No 1 golfer features heavily, as do his contemporaries at the very top of their games such as Ernie Els, Sergio Garcia, Justin Rose, Darren Clarke, Nick Faldo, Colin Montgomerie and Retief Goosen.

Golf World asks the questions you want the answers to, Golf World goes behind the scenes and into the homes of these superb athletes, and goes one step further - our writers actually tee it up with these greats.

Rounds are played with Nick Faldo, Tom Watson, Gary Player, and Darren Clarke as the writers discover just what it is like to engage the best in competition and their top coaches and psychologists feature as well. Butch Harmon, coach to Tiger Woods, and David Leadbetter, coach to many of the world's stars, reveal their thinking on the very best in the game today.

It's a rich mix. Be prepared for some big surprises!

On the road with Tiger

Being the best at golf is only a tiny part of the life of Tiger Woods. Five Golf World writers have followed his trail to bring you the perfect smiling PR machine, the globe-trotting pied piper, the jive-talking swing guru and the centre-piece of a multi-billion dollar industry.

Because with Tiger, nothing is as black and white as it seems...

PHOTOGRAPHY: ALLSPORT

The History Maker

By Jock Howard

PHOTOGRAPHY: PHIL SHELDON & ALLSPORT

Six down, 12 to go. The great Jack Nicklaus' major record beckons.

WHEN TIGER WOODS WAS FISHING IN Alaska in June, the week after playing in the Buick Classic, he looked up to see a bear staring at him from the other side of the river. Keeping an eye on the bear, Tiger cast his line out again. It sniffed the air a couple of times then started to wade across the water towards him. Woods reeled in fast and legged it.

It is ironic that Tiger was chased by a bear this year. He has, after all, been chasing one himself for the last 15. Shortly after his 10th birthday, Tiger (or Eldrick as he was then) picked up a copy of the American magazine *Golf Digest*. Inside he read a list of the all-time major championship leaders, and at the top was Jack Nicklaus, the Golden

The writing was on the wall. Well on the wall of Coca Cola tins, anyway.

Bear. Tiger ripped out the page and pinned it above the head-board of his bed.

Woods is obsessed with Jack Nicklaus. So much so he knows where Jack finished in the 1969 US Open (25th) and what colour socks he was wearing when he won his first Masters (blue). It would be no surprise if Tiger knew Jack's inside leg measurement (34³/₄, as it happens).

His one major goal in life is to beat the Golden Bear's major championship records. Why? Because major championships are acknowledged to be the measure of greatness in golf. Nicklaus has more than anyone else. Ergo, if Tiger wants to be remembered as the greatest player the planet has ever seen, he needs to beat Nicklaus' records.

Ask yourself why Tiger cried after winning last April's Masters. Let's face it, he's won lots of majors before, some of which have been a load more dramatic. And it wasn't as if no-one expected him to win this time, either. No, the reason his Nike cap became a receptacle for Tiger tears on the 18th green was that he realised he had done something the Golden Bear had never managed. "I started thinking I don't have any shots left to play," he said, still dewy eyed. "That's when I started getting a little emotional. I put the cap over my face so that when Phil [Mickelson] had finished, I was able to shake his hand." Tiger cried because he knew what it meant. "This year I understand," he said. "I've been around the block. I have a better appreciation for winning a major."

Nicklaus never won more than two majors in the same calendar year (although he did this five times). Nicklaus was never able to put all four trophies on

his coffee table at the same time. Tiger did precisely this at his home in Isleworth, on Monday 9th April, the day after he won the Masters. (At the 1972 Open Championship, Nicklaus came within a whisker of pulling it off but Lee Trevino beat him by one shot at Muirfield.)

Tiger had Georgia on his mind from the moment he shook Bob May's hand, after beating him in August 2000 in the USPGA Championship. He admitted he had been practising for many months specific shots which he thought he might need at the 2001 Masters. The high hook, which he played on the 13th tee in the final round, was a shot he had been perfecting in Hawaii in January. And two days after winning the Players' Championship, a week before the Masters, he was seen practising parachute lob shots beside the 1st green at Augusta National – at 6.05 am.

When Woods was crying at Augusta, Jack Nicklaus was several hundred miles away, after missing only his fourth cut in 42 appearances in the Masters. At his mansion in North Palm Beach, he was doing something he never usually does – watching golf on television. Before the event Jack disagreed with Tiger by saying the Grand Slam had to be executed in the same calendar year.

"I watched with great anticipation to see how it would unfold," said Nicklaus afterwards. "Is it a Grand Slam? I don't think it makes a difference.

What it's called is irrelevant. What he's done is what matters most, and what he's done is unbelievable. I call it the most remarkable feat I have ever seen or heard of in golf." So now Tiger has something else of Jack's. His seal of approval.

But if you ask Tiger about his obsession with Nicklaus, he becomes defensive. The goal to beat Nicklaus' 18 pro majors is a private goal which, like other private matters (girlfriends, flights on F-4 fighter jets, the firing of his agent and first caddie), Tiger likes to keep private. Try saying to him, (as one reporter did at the Open this summer): "Tiger, it is common knowledge that you are driven by emulating Jack Nicklaus. Is that a fact and can you talk about it a little bit?" He will stare you down.

"I don't want to be like Jack, no."
"In terms of emulating his record?"
"No, I don't want to emulate it."
"You would like to better it?"
"There is only one aspect I do want to emulate of his major championship record and that is his consistency – to put himself in there with a chance to win. Hopefully, I can put myself in there and win more titles. That would be the ideal situation. But in order to win as many major championships as Jack has won throughout his career, you have to be consistent and you have to put yourself there. You are not going to win every time. He finished second 19 times."

There is denial here. Tiger has always said: "My ambitions are very private and personal. I can't share them with you." And he means it. If he publicly announced his only ambition was to beat Jack's record, he would be putting additional pressure on himself. And yet, at last year's Open, he implied that if he could put himself in a position to win as many times as Nicklaus did he would win a bunch more than 18 majors.

After Tiger won his first Masters, Nicklaus famously said he would win as many Green Jackets as Arnold Palmer and he had won between them – which is 10. There are some who think Tiger can win as many major championships as Nicklaus and Palmer between them – which is 25. If that were to happen, who knows where Tiger could hide?

Right now he has escaped from the world on a scuba-diving holiday in the Bahamas. He loves it because, "what's great is the fish don't recognise me". If he won 25 major championships, the odd dottiback fish just might.

"I started getting a little emotional. I put the cap over my face so that when Phil Mickelson had finished I was able to shake his hand" Tiger Woods

TIGER WOODS
Born: December 30th 1975

Tiger as a pro (Major wins)
Year 1: 1997 **Won Masters**
Year 2: 1998 None
Year 3: 1999 **Won USPGA**
Year 4: 2000 **Won US Open, Open and USPGA**
Year 5: 2001 **Won Masters**

JACK NICKLAUS
Born: January 21st 1940

Jack as a pro aged 22 (Major wins and second places)
Year 1   1962   **Won US Open.**
Year 2:   1963   **Won Masters and USPGA.**
Year 3:   1964   Runner-up in Masters, Open and USPGA.
Year 4:   1965   **Won Masters.** Runner-up in USPGA.
Year 5:   1966   **Won Masters and Open.**
Year 6:   1967   **Won US Open.** Runner-up in Open.
Year 7:   1968   Runner-up in US Open and Open.
Year 8:   1969   None.
Year 9:   1970   **Won Open.**
Year 10: 1971   **Won USPGA.**
                   Runner-up in Masters and US Open.
Year 11: 1972   **Won Masters and US Open.** Runner-up in Open.
Year 12: 1973   **Won USPGA.**
Year 13: 1974   Runner-up in USPGA.
Year 14: 1975   **Won Masters and USPGA.**
Year 15: 1976   Runner-up in Open.
Year 16: 1977   Runner-up Masters and Open.
Year 17: 1978   **Won Open.**
Year 18: 1979   Runner-up in Open.
Year 19: 1980   **Won US Open and USPGA.**
Year 20: 1981   Runner-up in Masters.
Year 21: 1982   Runner-up in US Open.
Year 22: 1983   Runner-up in USPGA.
Year 23: 1984   None.
Year 24: 1985   None.
Year 25: 1986   **Won Masters.**

Hit the road, Jack...

Tiger has just finished his fifth full year as a professional and has captured six professional majors. He knows that – at this stage of his career – Jack had also won six. The difference is Tiger claimed his at the age of 25 years, three months and 9 days, whereas Nicklaus was 26 years, five months and 19 days. Nicklaus had finished runner-up four times after five years. Tiger has never been runner-up. Tiger is also aware that in Nicklaus' sixth year as a professional, he won his seventh major. So, in 2002, Tiger knows he must win at least one more to stay on equal terms. And so it goes on. In the next 10 years, Tiger must win another eight majors. By 2021 (by which time he will be 45) he must have won 18 or more. And then, and only then, can he hang up his Nike shoes.

	Jack	Tiger
First hit a golf ball	10 years	10 months
Broke 50 for nine holes	11 years	3 years
First broke par	aged 13	aged 13
First played in US Open	17	19
US Amateur victories	2	3
First round as a pro	74	67
First pro win	aged 22	aged 20
First major championship	22	21
Victories in first 72 tournaments	10	17
Most victories in a season	7	12
Majors played in (before career Grand Slam)	18	15

The Cash Cow

TV companies, tournaments, players, sponsors...everyone's milking Tiger.

By Steve Carr **PHOTOGRAPHY:** ALLSPORT

Unpaid ambassador Tiger Woods flies the flag for America on his trips abroad.

WHEN A COMPANY WHOSE REVENUE is $10 billion a year mentions an individual in its annual report, you better believe that person is like gold dust to them. Nike's 2001 statement has a small paragraph on the world number one that in part justifies to the shareholders the reported $100million five–year deal the company has pledged to Mr Woods. It also states the management think this is money well spent. It reads: "Okay, we can say a word or two about Tiger. C'mon, did you ever think you would see the day when the media would write headlines about some golfer changing the ball he plays? Then again, Tiger is not 'some golfer'. As only very few have done before him, he transcends his game, transcends sports, to affect dreams and engage cultures. He's the kind of athlete we love."

No wonder. Nike has posted increased revenues of 5.5% year on year, despite what can only be described as a difficult trading climate post September 11. Sales of its equipment lines, which include Tiger's Nike Tour Accuracy ball, have jumped 54.4%. And its share of the golf ball market has steadily improved in the past three years. The reason is not hard to fathom. A city analyst who two years ago predicted that Nike would be in the top five golf companies in the world by 2001 got it bang on, and he cited why he thought it would fly up the pecking order: "Tiger is the lightning rod in this business." And he didn't mean just Nike's business but the business of golf itself.

His estimated earnings for the past two years are $53million in 2000 and $57million in 2001 – staggering amounts for just one person to accrue. Compare those 'annual results' to those of one of the UK leisure industry's mega buck companies for the 12 months to July 2001: Manchester United plc made a profit of a mere £23million ($34million). Think of all those David

Beckham shirt sales, television rights, hyped-up ticket prices and the millions of fans worldwide that clamour to be part of the Red economy. One golfer banks almost 50% more.

Tiger will earn $60 million without blinking. He is almost recession proof. Because most of his earnings are off-course deals bound into contracts for up to five years, he will keep on bankrolling his cash. He is the benchmark Tiger Economy, which the dictionary states is: 'A term originally used to describe a rapidly-growing economy in the Far East, but now applies to any economy where growth prospects are thought to be high'.

Woods has 'only' earned $6million on the course this year, about 10% of his total revenue, so his outlook is rosy even if he doesn't play next year. But if he does, despite the threat of recession, then he is still set to earn at least $12 million in appearance fees. Currently the market rate is around $2million if you take the lure to the Deutsche Bank Open to be a sign of the times.

While he is feathering his own nest rather nicely, his presence and super stardom is also lining the pockets of many others. Although the PGA Tour don't like to admit it, Tiger has been mostly responsible for the hiking of prize money on the US Tour. When the TV deal was renegotiated in the late 1990s, total prize money spiralled from $69million in 1996 to $169million in 2000. "We estimate the total purse for 2002 will be $200million," says a tour spokesperson.

It is not just in America that the upsurge in money has been noted, thanks in part to the new kudos Tiger has brought to the game. The European Tour has seen vast hikes in prize money over the last few years. In 1996 only eight players broke the 500,000 Euro barrier and it was still only 14 in 1999, but in 2001 39 players have surpassed that figure. But it is not just the top that

have been beneficiaries. The money you needed to retain your all-exempt playing card on the European Tour has risen from 74,000 Euros in 1995 to 83,000 in 1998 to a whopping 161,000 in 2001.

Don't the players just love it too. Stewart Cink was asked in the aftermath of Tiger's historic Masters win in April whether he and others had picked the wrong time to play pro golf. He laughed: "The tournament purses keep going up. I think I was born at exactly the right time."

The spin-off world of Tiger Woods is a booming business. Online auction house eBay currently has 1,989 Tiger Woods items up for auction. The highest bid for one was $14,000 for a signed collectable card. In March, a similar card was sold for $125,000. Signed Augusta National flags from 2001 are a snip at $4,000.

US business magazine Forbes produced in June its list of the world's top 100 money-earning celebrities. Tiger was only surpassed by Tom Cruise, who nipped ahead of him on account of the amount of magazine covers he had appeared on in the last 12 months. Tiger ranked 7th in money earned, one place above Steven Spielberg, but headed the list of TV and radio hits and press clippings with a massive 47,149. There were only 20 Blue Chip Company CEOs above him in the salary category.

Entering just his sixth year as a professional, Tiger is now the axis about which the golf industry revolves. If he were to spurn his home Tour tomorrow and start his own, the sponsors would surely flock to him. And if you still doubt that he moves in powerful circles, swallow this announcement, if you will, before Tiger's press conference after winning that earth-moving Masters last April. "Apologies for the delay, ladies and gentlemen," said Augusta National's Billy Payne. "President Bush just called to congratulate Tiger."

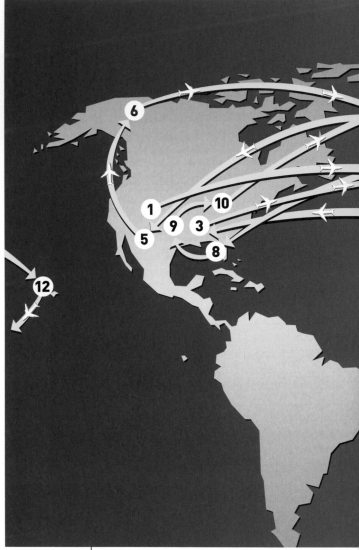

Pied Piper
By Peter Masters

They say it's a world tour now, but golf has never had a globetrotter quite like Mr Woods.

Anyone playing at home is tough to beat, it's just that for Tiger, at home happens to be planet earth.

His yearly schedule, primed at the Orlando, Florida, office of his management company IMG then sent out to field staff around the world, reads like a blueprint for a finely-tuned set of military manoeuvres. For all the qualities to which Tiger has earned the tag 'phenomenon', it is his stamina and commitment that is top of the list.

He is not just the best player in the world, he is a missionary, a pied piper of golf who sees his task in life as going far beyond any personal objectives of becoming a better player than Jack Nicklaus.

"I like to play overseas," he says. "I enjoy seeing different environments. I think it's great to grow the game that way. I think you do yourself an injustice by not playing overseas and developing your game."

When Woods was in Dubai, he approached Padraig Harrington and asked him about his schedule. The Irishman mentioned having just been to Singapore and Tiger's interest grew. He had never been to Singapore and wanted to know all about it. There aren't too many Americans with that attitude. But then again Tiger is not an all-American. Ask him about his roots and he describes himself as Cablinasian, a mixture of Caucasian, Black, American Indian and Asian.

He has always seen himself in global terms. His father Earl once declared "Tiger will do more than any other human in history to change the course of humanity." Earl had never envisaged merely a golfing icon, more a global one in the context of Mandela and Gandhi.

This year Woods has circumnavigated the globe and he kicks off the 2002 season with his first visit to New Zealand. He does all this, crossing time zones, and is still able to walk onto the course and win.

It is as if Woods has no nationality. The Chinese welcomed him with open arms at Mission Hills where, in an exhibition match, he was beaten on the last hole. "Did you miss that putt on purpose. Was it a gesture of good will?" they asked. "It was just a bad putt," smiled Tiger.

With his punishing schedule, the biggest threat could be one of burn out. Woods spoke about the problem earlier this season. "I think I played too much at the end of last year. I played eight consecutive weeks, on four continents and travelled more than 27,000 miles."

It is not too often that Tiger gets anything wrong on or off the course. It is often said in golf that a bad shot is hitting the big ball before the small one. But in Tiger's case, no sportsman has ever hit the big ball harder.

The incredible journey
Tracing the Tiger trail throughout 200

1 **US Tour**
Mercedes, Phoenix, AT&T, Buick Invitational, LA Open

2 **European Tour**
Dubai Desert Classic

3 **US Tour**
Bay Hill, Players, Masters.
In a four week break, he attends clinics in Alabama and California as well as his Tiger Jam concert in Las Vegas. Byron Nelson

4 **European Tour**
Deutsche Bank Open

ILLUSTRATION: GRAHAM GACHES

Tiger's first trip overseas took him to the Dubai desert.

Pomp and ceremony on his arrival in China, is followed...

by a junior clinic under the watchful gaze of a capacity crowd.

⑤ US Tour
Memorial, US Open, Buick Classic.
Opens Nike's new conference centre in Illinois and signs 250 autographs for the Upper Deck Trading Co.

⑥ US Tour
Western Open
He is chased by a brown bear when on a fishing holiday in Alaska with Mark O'Meara and John Cook.

⑦ European Tour
Open
O'Meara and David Duval joins him for a week prior to the Open at the K Club in Ireland fishing in the Liffey and playing golf at Waterville.

⑧ US Tour
USPGA, NEC Invitational.
He drove for 13 hours in his journey alone back to Orlando. Then after winning the Battle of Bighorn with Annika Sorenstam. He attended his fourth junior clinic.

⑨ US Tour
National Car Rental
The September 11 atrocities lead to a five week break, the longest of his career. He records a video of condolences for the employees of American Express, plays a quiet 54 holes with Michael Jordan and records live television interviews with Oprah Winfrey and Larry King.

⑩ US Tour
Tour Championship.
He is invited with Mark O'Meara to play the new altered layout at Augusta.

⑪ Prior to the World Cup in Japan, he gives an exhibition and clinic at Mission Hills in China.

⑫ He stops off at Hawaii on the way home for the Grand Slam of Golf. He then plays a skins match in California and his own tournament the Williams World Challenge in December.

⑬ Tiger kicks off 2002 at the New Zealand Open in January.

The Inventor

By Paul Mahoney

Different shots. Different language. Different planet.

THE BOY'S GOT A GREAT ENGINE. He'll run all day. He lollipops his oppo for fun, knocks a great ball into the big lad at the back stick who's left his marker for dead, and tucks it away sweet into the top corner. The keeper never had a prayer. Blindin' finish. Footballers started this nonsense and Big Ron Atkinson is the daddy.

The best most golfers could come up with was: I hit some good drives, found some fairways and holed a coupla putts. Appreciate it, Dougie. Okay, it's not clever, it's not even stupid. But at least it's the Queen's English – even if it is mind-numbingly dull.

But Tiger Woods has ripped up the golfing dictionary and reinvented the oldest sporting language in the world. Not only does he play a different game to his peers, he talks a different game, too.

No-one has a bloody clue what he's talking about half the time but no-one has the courage to be the first to ask. He's the Big Ron of golf and it's safer to nod along with the crowd and pretend we're all on the same wavelength as the master, much as we did in French lessons at school.

Tiger doesn't strike the ball, or hit it or draw it. He grinds, jerks and smokes. Sounds more like the stage directions to a cheap skin flick. He comes from a fairly privileged army influenced background but uses the language of inner city ghetto street gangs and is clearly influenced by the lyrics of his favourite musician, the rap artist Shaggy. Tiger really is not on the same planet as the diamond-patterned sweater brigade.

This Tiger rap has been creeping ever more into his vocabulary. This year he has obviously been buying a stack of CDs and is all but breaking out into song. At the 10th hole in the final round of his historic win at Augusta, he was faced with a 3-wood shot out of rough to a green that he couldn't see. Standing no more than 10 yards yards from the galleries straining over the ropes, he drilled it to 15 feet from the pin. If this act alone is not out-of-this-world enough for you, listen to his post mortem of the shot in his press conference. "I had 253 to the hole, coming out of the rough," he said. Okay, so far. "I choked down on it, just tried to hit a little three-quarter 3-wood and just chip it up there somewhere. I raked across it and hit a little bleeder." I beg your pardon. Does that mean he walloped a noisy kid in the crowd? Or did he cut himself? We've no idea what he means but, for those who witnessed the shot, it sounds sort of like what happened in real time without the commentary. All we can do is fill in the blanks, read between the lines, get by the best we can.

"I really hit good shots but they were not stoning," he said at the Masters. "They were not kick-ins." That's just Tiger rap for: "My shots weren't landing close to the pin and I was leaving rather lengthy putts." Probably. When he realised that he had no chance of winning the US Open in June he said afterwards: "You can't bag it. You can't dog it." You have to admit, you might not be able to fathom a word of what he's saying but it sounds a hell of a lot more fruity, more street cred, more yoof-oriented than: "You can't give up."

This rapping is essentially an American thing. He dumbs it down (or perhaps dumbs it up) for the more sedate, traditional British audience which likes its English spoke right good and proper. Tiger is much less in yer face on his visits to Europe. But, rest assured (or be warned), like all things American, we'll get a fistful of Tiger's new golf rap soon enough. At Royal Lytham this year he warmed up with an explanation of how on the 10th, "I got steep on it and shut it down. I was trying to hit a nice soft sweeper." Answers on a postcard, please.

Talking about his early days on tour, Tiger admits "my mechanics weren't anywhere near as sound as they are now." Probably because he owns more Buicks these days and can afford the best engineers. But that's just how Tiger sees his game – it's a machine that needs oiling, tweaking and polishing. While Colin Montgomerie rarely practises, the World No.1 is obsessive about his golf swing, and his attention to detail about how it works is phenomenal. Again, he has developed a bizarre fascination with the mechanics of hitting a ball with a stick.

On the eve of the US Open at Pebble Beach in 2000, Tiger complained to his coach Butch Harmon

In his quest for golfing greatness Tiger has a tremendous work ethic with coach Butch Harmon.

about his putting. "The ball wasn't turning over the way I would like to see it roll," he said. The ball is round, it rolls, he can spot a difference? Excuse me! Oh, he won of course, taking just 110 putts which was 6th best. "When I need any extra 20 yards," he explains about his long game this time, "I've found that by snapping my left leg straight, my hips clear faster and speed up the movement of my shoulders, arms and legs." (*Golf World* accepts no liability for the maiming of any readers daft enough to try this manoeuvre at their local driving range.)

Asked to nominate his best shot of the year in the majors, Tiger picked his tee shot at Augusta's 13th on Masters Sunday. "I had to step up there and hit the big slinger," he said. Tiger says he is searching for a golf game that can co-exist with what he wants in his mind and Fred Couples reckons he knows where Tiger is coming from – sort of. "He's one of a kind," he says. "He's so good you don't understand him because he's so good." Sorry, Freddie, could you repeat that? Slowly.

PHOTOGRAPHY: ALLSPORT

"I got steep on it and shut it down. I was trying to hit a nice soft sweeper."
Answers on a postcard, please.

Even the distances he hits the ball are unreal – judge them against yourself
(average hits including roll)

Tiger's distances		low h'cap	mid	high
Driver	290	240	220	200
3-wood	260	225	205	180
2-iron	225	210	NA	NA
3-iron	215	195	180	170
4-iron	205	185	170	160
5-iron	190	175	160	150
6-iron	180	165	150	140
7-iron	170	155	140	130
8-iron	160	145	130	120
9-iron	150	135	120	110
PW	135	125	110	100
SW	115	105	90	75
LW	105			

The Smooth Talker

Silly questions from dumb reporters. Tiger Woods always has the answers.

By Bill Elliott

THERE IS ONLY ONE ANNOUNCEMENT guaranteed to cause the world's media to stampede at tournaments. It is when "Tiger Woods is in the Interview Area" squawks over the public address system. This is when The Phenom plays his other 'A game' – the schmoozer.

When Tiger made his first appearance at a major UK press conference at the Open in 1995 at St Andrews, he was still an amateur. But clearly he had been coached and briefed for the occasion. There was a natural teenage gaucheness about him but he had either learned to make eye contact with any questioner or he was instinctively good at it. Many young sportsmen are too frequently thrown into the cauldron minus any real preparation. Witness the problems Justin Rose encountered when he left the amateur world. He has now learned the tough way how to deal with men old enough to be his dad, some of whom are planting carefully contrived questions in an attempt to trick him into a verbal indiscretion.

Tiger, too, used to be vulnerable. Three months after turning professional he spent several days in the company of an American lifestyle magazine, who then repeated a couple of dirty jokes he had told them in the back of a cab.

It damaged Tiger's clean-cut All-American image, upset his sponsors and it taught him a valuable lesson: trust no-one.

This is as sad as it is sadly necessary. Since this low point Tiger has turned himself into one of the slickest interviewees in sport. Quicker than anyone else he has realised the mass media press conference is a bear-pit and so he throws the animals a few buns now and then to keep them happy. Not for him the taciturn

Q: Do you ever wake up in the middle of the night and say: "Whoa, how did I do that? Can I do it again?" Tiger Woods press conference, US Open, Tuesday, June 12th, 2001

A: Usually when I wake up in the middle of the night, it's to do something else (laughter). **You ask amazing questions.**

approach of Nick Faldo in his prime, much less the monosyllabic yes/no period of Mark James. Tiger knows he cannot beat the press and he knows also that it is through the press that the world learns more about him as a golfer and a person.

He is, usually, courteous and charming. He looks you in the eye when you ask a question and if you have a name badge on he often prefaces his answer by using your name which, of course, can be hugely flattering. It is simple PR but this silky technique works on many a hardened hack. Even if he chooses to begin his response with a put-down – always embarrassing in front of hundreds of your peers – he instantly dilutes the effect by grinning broadly to defuse a potentially unpleasant situation.

He has wit, too. In a packed press conference after completing his Slam at Augusta this year, an American (naturally) piped up with this schmaltzy question: "When Pete Rose (a bigshot baseball player) hit his record run he said he looked to the sky and saw his father's face. When you holed your final putt today did you see anything, was there a moment of gravity for you?"

Tiger screwed up his face in mock concentration and thought for a few seconds, then fixed his questioner with hard eyes and replied: "No". He did not add to this answer but just as the reporter began to

squirm, Tiger did his big smiley thing again – and everyone, including the squirmee, laughed.

A few minutes later at Augusta some bright spark – American again – asked what Tiger would say to Bobby Jones if he bumped

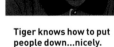

Tiger knows how to put people down...nicely.

into the great man back in the clubhouse. Given that Jones has been dead for a while now this was a seriously strange enquiry. Woods, however, did not bat an eyelid as he responded: "I'd ask him how the heck he got back here." Alright, it is not Bob Hope, or even maybe Jimmy Tarbuck, but it is sharp. And most of all it is quick and, under the pressure of a mass press conference, it is genuinely funny.

But ask him a challenging question and he will treat it with genuine intelligence. Tiger steers clear of individual interviews but it is possible to slip through the security guys on to the practice ground. Tiger was practising wedge shots at the US Open two years ago when I managed to get six feet behind him where I stood watching, saying nothing. Eventually his caddie looked at me as though I'd been fetched up by a dog and snarled: "Waddya want?"

I replied in a deliberately over the top Queen's

Trained in the art of public speaking.

English accent: "That's awfully sweet of you to ask but it's actually your employer I wish to speak to."

The ploy worked and Tiger's lips twitched into a smile. After hitting a few more wedges just to establish rank, he turned, grinned, and asked what he could do for me. I asked him if he felt players should be paid to play in the Ryder Cup. His reply was typically forthright. Yes, he did, and what's more he felt a fee of around $200,000 would be about right. This money, he said, would be donated to a charity of the player's choice and no cash would go into any private pocket.

It made a story that raced around the United States and began a prolonged set of negotiations between the players and the PGA of America. It ended with Tiger getting exactly what he wanted. I had been lucky and asked the right question at the right time and Tiger had used me to fire an opening shot in a battle he was determined to win. Fair enough, I was using him to get a story. This system of mutually acceptable 'abuse' is the way it is. Tiger Woods, however, has worked out probably better than anyone else just how to use it to his advantage.

Even under a barrage of questions from the world's press, Tiger keeps smiling.

PHOTOGRAPHY:
PHIL SHELDON

The dumb questions that demand smart answers

THE CHARMING, DISARMING MR ELDRICK (TIGER) WOODS

MASTERS SATURDAY
Q: With all the historical implications of tomorrow, are you thinking about that at all or just shutting it out?
A: I haven't thought about it. Sorry. (laughter)...

Q: ...Come on. Give us something better than that. This is something a lot of us may never see again in our lifetime if you win again tomorrow?
A: I hope you live a little longer then. (more laughter).

Q: Who do you think is to blame for the expectations maybe getting a little bit out of hand? Was it us? Was it you?
A: Well, I know that answer. (laughter). Don't look at me. (more laughter). You know, I think probably both. (smiles all round).

MASTERS SUNDAY
Q: How long can this winning streak go on?
A: I don't know. We'll find out in June. (smiles).

Q: What's your jacket size?
A: About this big. (laughter).

Q: Now that you have done it (four majors in a row), what do you want to call it?
A: I'll let you guys decide. You are very creative.

Q: Are you going to do anything cool with the four major trophies?
A: What do you want me to do with them? I know what your mind would do with them. (laughter).

US OPEN TUESDAY
Q: Do you prepare differently for a major than for a regular event?
A: I do but I don't.

Q: Do you ever wake up in the middle of the night and say: "Whoa, how did I do that? Can I do it again?"
A: Usually when I wake up in the middle of the night, it's to do something else. (laughter).

US OPEN SUNDAY
Q: Tiger, coming in as overwhelming favourite, is this the most disappointed you've been after a major in a long time?
A: Considering I won the last four – yes.

This is the last time you'll see

Big Easy

in an Ernie Els headline

Why the World No.3 and Open Champion wants to dump his nick-name, how he plans to attack Tiger, who saved his career this year, and where he loves living most.

WORDS: **Paul Mahoney** PHOTOGRAPHY: **James Cheadle** (portraits), **Getty Images** (action)

STEALING THE Open Championship claret jug from Ernie Els' house couldn't be easier. It's not imprisoned in a reinforced steel cabinet under lock and key. There are no trip wires, laser beams or pulse rate detectors. No secret codes to crack. No tooled up heavies. No barbed wire. No bother. A small stepladder or a bunk up from an accomplice gets you over the wooden gates at the bottom of his driveway deep in the heart of the Wentworth Estate in Millionaire's Valley, Surrey. A 40-yard dash up the path brings you to the front of the de luxe Hansel & Gretel cottage.

And there it sits, sunlight caressing its unmistakable curvaceous waistline and pouting lip: the world's most priceless golf trophy is right in front of you, naked, on a chest of drawers inside the window right of the door, bold as brass (solid as silver, actually), the ultimate wow factor for visiting friends, postmen, media and burglars. It's just begging to be nicked.

A swift chuck of a half brick, hidden in your dungarees, would set up the easiest smash-and-grab of your tinkering career. Then all you'd have to do, as the alarm bell shatters the birdsong, is scarper. The perfect crime. Except Ernie has a couple of home-made security surprises. Firstly, the path is awash with that expensive gravel that posh hotels employ retired gardeners to rake. Walking on it announces your arrival like a heavy-booted army square bashing on a parade ground of Rice Krispies. Worse still, this explosion of snaps, crackles and pops triggers the over-enthusiastic and, frankly, terrifying arrival of George and Zsa Zsa – butler and maid they most certainly are not. Prepare for death by slobber courtesy of two monster-sized St Bernards that are more pit pony than dog.

Even if you survive their over-amorous attack, you might still be unlucky to find that Mr Els is at home – and he's 15 stone and 6 ft 3in. Now he might be softly spoken, laid back to the point of horizontal (according to his wife Liezl) and slow moving but he's not the sort of fellow you'd want to be collared by hoofing it with his crown jewels. Those enormous knarled mountaineer's fists could cause serious internal damage

if you riled The Big Easy to become The Big Smack In The Mouth.

This whole scenario, worryingly, occurred to me when I visited Els at home in late August. Probably been watching too many late-night Jimmy Cagney heist movies. It was just so shocking to see the Open Championship claret jug so openly displayed.

Even if you do make good your escape, your fence (not the wooden kind) would take no pleasure in telling you that you had snatched the wrong blinkin' jug. You see there are two on display chez Els at the moment. One is the 'second' original (brought out of its padded box and placed on the coffee table for Golf World's visit), made in 1927, which Els will return when he defends his title next July at Royal St George's in Kent. The 'first' original trophy really is under lock and key in the Royal & Ancient glass cabinet at St Andrews. It turns out the jug in the Els' front window is the two-thirds size replica that Ernie gets to keep. An expensive fake, if you like. The golfing equivalent of a Dubai market Rolex.

Els clearly has not smelt a whiff of any impending attempted robbery. He is looking more relaxed than he

"My confidence is nine out of 10 now.
I feel I am a force to be reckoned with again –
especially in the majors"

has been all year. And so he should be. He is at home, Liezl is just a few weeks away from delivering their second child (baby Ben arrived in October; a brother for three-year-old Samantha). And he is the Open Champion.

This season has been quite a ride for the 33-year-old – and Els shot from desperation to jubilation in under a week in July. He grimaces and glances Heavenward recalling the state of his game and his mind at the Scottish Open at Loch Lomond, the full dress rehearsal for what would turn out to be his starring role in the Greatest Show In Golf the following week at Muirfield. "Oh My God," he winces then

Els wins his first Open Championship. "It means a lot more to me than the Order of Merit or the World Rankings."

half-smiles, shaking his head. "I was totally out of sorts. I was losing it a bit there. I was nowhere. I played awful. The worst I'd played all year. I even considered going home to take two days off before the Open, just to get away from the game. But then I got in my car with Ricky (Els' caddie) after my final round and drove straight to Greywalls (the famous hotel next to the course at Muirfield. We went out for a couple pints, had dinner, woke up the next morning and said, right, let's go and sort it out. And everybody was there."

Everybody, crucially, means swing coach David Leadbetter and mind guru Jos Vanstiphout. Leadbetter tweaked this, fine-tuned that. Vanstiphout poured five-star premium oil over rusty cogs. But Els' engine just wouldn't jump-start. "I was still nowhere on Monday and Tuesday." On Tuesday afternoon Els gave a press conference and looked frustrated and irritated and sounded down beat. "Shots aren't coming out the way I'm visualising them," he admitted. "I can't get my game going…When I've played well, Tiger has still beaten me… Maybe I'm not good enough – who knows?" He was clearly low on confidence and the daily newspapers wrote him off saying he had all but conceded victory to Tiger Woods. Most players, regardless of their form or class, feel the need to straight bat questions to avoid such morale-sapping headlines. But Els, perhaps caught off-guard suffering his inner turmoil, was refreshingly honest. "I just wasn't going to sit there and tell everyone my chances were great. That's just bullshit," he explains. "I felt the way I said it. Maybe it was the wrong thing to say, but I said it."

He needn't have worried. That undefinable missing link clicked into place on Wednesday morning. It proved to be the pivotal moment of his week, his year, probably even his career and the rest of his life. "I started hitting the ball well and I felt I could compete," he remembers. "And the rest is history," he says proudly but modestly like all he'd done was go out and win the Wentworth Club monthly medal.

But he can't contain his delight and wonder of what he says is his greatest achievement. He admits he is still buzzing inside. Almost more so than in July, now that what he has achieved has sunk in. The World No.3 and two-time US Open champion was already respected as one of the finest players and nicest people on tour. But even he can tell that spectators and players look at him differently now. Such is the impact of winning the oldest major of the year. But, you won't be surprised to hear, he says his life hasn't changed at all. Just how much life needs to change for someone who already owns a second home at Lake Nona in Florida and a ranch in South Africa? He hasn't bought a new house (three's plenty, it seems) or a new car but says: "I definitely feel different but it's hard to describe how." He pauses, searching for the right words, then announces: "I believe again!" He laughs at his mock revivalist born-again sinner's confession. There is, however, a joyous relief in his voice, eyes and body language. Hallelujah, Els is golf's Lazarus. "My confidence has been only about seven out of 10 for the past few years," he says, baring his soul. That

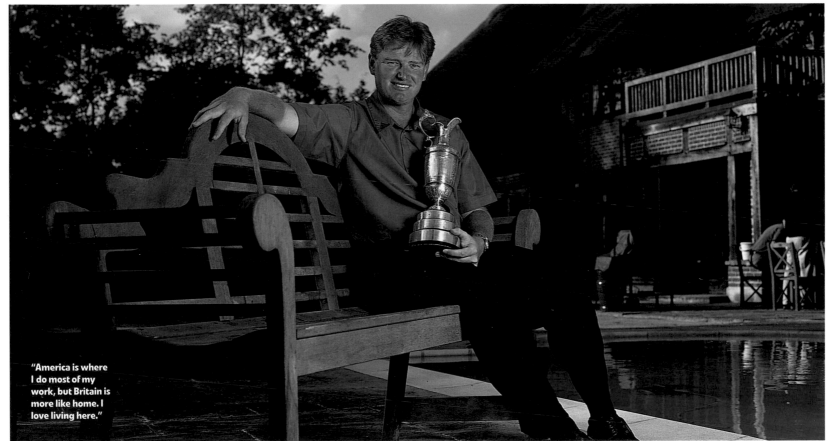

"America is where I do most of my work, but Britain is more like home. I love living here."

gives you an insight into how high standards need to be for these top players.

Those doubters who still think Els' bottle is as steady as a chocolate teapot on a jelly stove had better sit down. "My confidence is nine out of 10 now. I feel I am a force to be reckoned with again – especially in the majors. I really want to take advantage of my mental attitude at the moment." And that includes dumping his Big Easy label. He turned up his nose and pooh-poohed this tired cliché. It clearly irks him a little. "I don't pay a lot of attention to it," he says. "My sponsors dreamed it up. Okay, I'm a big guy. And I guess somebody thinks I swing slow and easy. But I think I swing quickly." You can see the Big Easy persona melting before you as a steely determination burns through his eyes. Perhaps next season Tiger can expect to be shown the Big E instead.

"If you want to play at the highest level, you've got to have a certain amount of competitiveness," Els says in answer to those who question the sharpness of his cutting edge. "I believe I have that. In a way, I may be blessed that it doesn't come out in my appearance. But I know it's there. I felt it at the Open again." You can see now why he has grown tired of those Big Easy headlines. They are not necessarily accurate, they don't reflect his ambitions and they certainly don't do his competitive aura any favours. They suggest he is not a serious contender.

"Okay, I'm a big guy. And I guess somebody thinks I swing slow and easy. But I think I swing quickly"

"When you lose a tournament like the Open (Els double bogied the 16th to throw away his stranglehold on the trophy) and then you've got just two holes to pull out something, to salvage it, there has got to be some kind of intensity and guts. There is something there; I know it's there," he says again, convincingly. "I've just got to do it more often." There is seriousness in his tone. Els is desperate and determined to build on his rediscovered passion and aggression.

But , you may be surprised to hear, Woods isn't his target. In the midst of his major drought, Els told me "being No.1 does not mean as much to me as it does to Tiger." But now, after winning the Open and stating, "I've got a lot more fire back," Els admits nothing has changed. "Winning the Open means a lot more to me than the Order of Merit or the World Rankings. You go down in history for being Open champion. If I win the Grand Slam next year, I still won't be No.1 because Tiger is so far ahead. I just want to win tournaments and majors. Whatever comes with that will come. I don't even want to think about being No.1."

No so long ago, such a statement could be conceived as revealing an inferiority complex; putting a poor spin on reality to ease the pain that there is somebody out there that has his number – and everybody else's for that matter. It could even be called defeatist.

Els and Phil Mickelson took flak for not taking a tough enough fight to Woods who won the US Open easily in June at Bethpage, New York. Gary Player (one of Els' mentors) and Jack Nicklaus were the mud-chuckers. Some of it was still sticking to Els at the start of the week of the British Open and he admitted it hurt. After the Open, Jos Vanstiphout, Els' mind doctor announced that his patient had cured his Tigeritis. Certainly, today, there is less stress in Els' voice when discussing the World No.1, less irritation at what he once blasted "more damn Tiger questions", and a more positive outlook on their rivalry.

"If I can keep my confidence high, the better I can play, and the more fun we are going to have on Sunday afternoons – because that's where Tiger is going to be. He is beating me 70% of the time but the more I play in that circle with him, the more I can compete rather than being just a flash in the pan." A statement that shows ambition yet throws light on the fact that Els is aware that if he doesn't successfully challenge Woods, then his Open victory could well be seen as just a flash in the pan.

The man who Els credits greatly with helping to turn his career around is the chain-smoking Vanstiphout, a former newspaper salesman now getting rich with his self-taught DIY sports psychology. When they first met, about 18 months ago, Vanstiphout chastised Els for being a lazy slob who wasn't hungry any more. They had a blazing row but Els was impressed with the Belgian's no-nonsense approach and they struck a deal. Vanstiphout told Els the best way to beat Woods was to forget him – which might explain Els' statement that he's not interested in chasing Woods to become No.1. Understandably, Els is reluctant to discuss exactly what the two of them talk about, except to say Vanstiphout keeps things simple. "It's all about getting the ball from A to B," Els says, as if reading from the Gospel according to Saint Jos. "It's not a four-and-a-half hour round; it's a five-minute round. He wants me to concentrate on every shot."

Els' new-found aggression on the course coupled with his inner karma at home and within himself seems to be working. He ended his season with a fourth World Matchplay title at Wentworth, thrashing Colin Montgomerie in an early round before overcoming Sergio Garcia in the final. He then flew to Atlanta for the US Tour Championship in October before heading to Home No.1 in South Africa and a well-earned chill out on the beach. He says he loves both US and European Tours and will always be a world player (Els kicks off his 2003 season at the Johnnie Walker Classic in Perth). But he feels more at home in Britain. While he has tempered his negative obsession with Woods, he is still irritated by his lack of recognition on the US Tour, despite winning their Open twice. While the more volcanic Monty and Garcia soak up the abuse and adoration of the galleries, the even-keeled Els goes about his business as World No.3 virtually unnoticed by fans and media alike. "I have felt Americans aren't interested in me," he says shrugging his shoulders. "I don't know why. But they definitely want to promote their own players more. That's one of the reasons why I feel more at home in Britain."

Walking out into his back garden, Els says Wentworth reminds him of his home when he was growing up. There is open space, tennis courts and a swimming pool. The food is similar; the children will go to school here and the British play the same sport as South Africans. "We love spending time in America, too," he says. "But we feel more European. America is where I do most of my work but Britain is more like home." He is, by his own admission, one of us and we'll gladly embrace him. So the next Brit to win a major? Could well be Surrey's Ernie Els. Or, failing that, Hampshire's Justin Rose. And even he was born in Johannesburg.

" My shot of the year "

2002 Open Championship
13th green, final round

MUIRFIELD, JULY 21: Ernie Els is three shots clear with six holes to play. On the tee of the 191-yard par three he feels he is between clubs. He chooses a 7-iron but hits it too hard. His ball flies left into the deepest bunker. It is the very swing fault he has been fighting all season. The bunker shot that followed was a tremendous recovery under intense pressure.

❝This shot was more difficult than the one I had at the 18th in the play-off. I had more room to work the ball on the 18th. I just had to keep my balance. But the one on the 13th was tougher. I'm still amazed I got it out there – and I almost holed it! It reminded me a lot of the Road Hole bunker on the 17th at St Andrews. As I climbed into the bunker I told Ricky, my caddie, I was going to hit it as hard as I could. I felt I had a chance to get it out with my 60 degree wedge. It came out perfect. I was in the same bunker on the second day but left it in the sand. That was my practice shot for Sunday! I felt, after that sand save, this was my tournament to win.❞

He dines with presidents, flies his own jet, sails one of the world's biggest yachts and has banked more cash than he cares to add up. He's won two majors (and blown seven) and is still expanding his business empire after 25 years on tour. Life must be perfect for...

Saint Greg

WORDS: JOCK HOWARD **PORTRAITS:** JAMES CHEADLE

You know something big is about to strike.

First come the rumours and the idle chit-chat. "Someone told me he dyes his hair?" "I've heard he's going to arrive on the back lawn in his Bell Ford 30 chopper."

Then there is a frenzy of activity as everyone battens down the hatches. The bellboy at the front door madly sweeps two sad looking leaves off the mat while the girl on reception stabs the edges of her mouth with pink lipstick.

And finally, sweeping into view around a corner in the front drive, he appears...

Greg Norman has arrived. He is here at the 'K' Club, south-west of Dublin, with his wife, Laura, and two kids, Morgan-Leigh (20) and Gregory (16) – they will do a bit of sight-seeing, maybe go to Italy and Spain. Greg will open his much talked about new course at Doonbeg, on the west coast of Ireland, and play in a couple of small tournaments – one of which is at Muirfield.

An hour and a half earlier, the Normans had touched down at Dublin airport in their very own Boeing 737. Inside, this has been converted to look more like Buckingham Palace than an aeroplane. There are beds and sofas, video machines and a bar. The staff (two pilots, an engineer and a hostess) are full-time employees and have been left at the airport to service the aircraft.

Norman emerges from the first car in the cavalcade, a shock of blond hair, sun-tanned and smiling despite the jet lag. (Maybe you don't get jet lag if you cross the Atlantic in your own double-bed.) Behind him is a fleet of identical cars, carrying his luggage. Whoever packs for this guy has his work cut out. If the President of the United States had just arrived, he would not have had more luggage. Nor caused more excitement. Indeed, idle observers going about their chores have to take care not to get sucked in to the back-draught.

Norman is not your communal garden golfer. No one who has ever played the game (with the possible exception of a guy called Eldrick) has such an aura about him. Even at the age of 47 (the crow's feet around both eyes are beginning to give away the fact that the Great White Shark has reached middle age) it is still impossible to exaggerate his ability to turn heads. If he walks into a room you can instantly feel his presence by the ripples in the water.

So, why does a man who has everything, still keep moving and shaking? Why doesn't he just cash in his chips, do all the things he really wants to do, and stay at home with his wife and kids? Why the drive to add to the hundreds of millions he already has?

"I guess it's just my nature," he says. "I've never been a couch potato or a follower. I learned early on in my life if you want something you've got to go and get it. I like to work hard. I guess the big question is how much is enough isn't it? I've got friends in their 60s who are a heck of a lot wealthier than me, and I ask them 'Why do you keep doing this?' And they turn to me and say 'Why do you keep doing it?' I say 'What are you going to do with all that money?' And they look at me and say 'Well, what are you going to do with all your money?' If I see something I want to achieve I go after it.

That's just the way I am."

Greg Norman swims in influential circles. He's a friend of President George Bush and has had dinner with Nelson Mandela. When he was President, Bill Clinton infamously came to stay at his home at Hobe Sound in Florida, and tore knee ligaments while being shown to his quarters.

Because of the company Norman keeps, and because some people are jealous of him, and because he plays only about five events on the regular tour nowadays, and because he felt many of his peers let him down when he tried to start a world tour in 1994, Norman doesn't mix much with other tour pros. He goes to Mexico once a year at Christmas with Steve Elkington where they shoot birds, and in the summer they fish and go hunting in the Rocky Mountains. He sees a bit of Raymond Floyd and his family because Floyd has always been a father figure to him. But otherwise, tour professionals and even players like Nick Price (who he was big buddies with at one time) are lucky if they get a Christmas card from the Great White.

Because of his success, jealousy is something he has had to deal with throughout his career. When he first arrived at a tournament in Florida in his helicopter some years ago, he could feel the envious looks on the practice range and in the locker room. "It bothered me for a while," he admitted recently in an American magazine, "but you have to let it go. If guys are jealous of my helicopter, they should go work harder and get their own. It's not like somebody just gave me a helicopter. I worked my ass off to get it."

Norman's business empire is huge and diverse, but the cornerstones are based on growing wine and grass and designing clothes and golf courses. A World Series and a Super Bowl have been held on Greg Norman grass. Everything (probably even the grass) comes with several multi-coloured Great White Shark logos. Indeed, when you are talking to him, there is a terrible temptation to play 'find the shark' and see how many logos you can spot swimming around different parts of his anatomy – a bit like those games in kids' books where you have to spot 10 rabbits hidden in a picture of a country scene. During my hour, I found eight.

"I'm going to write my biography soon," he says, crossing his legs, and revealing another shark on the bottom of his leather shoe, "because I do get irritated by the speculation about my business interests. People ring up and want to know how much I'm worth. But that's the beauty of being a private company – it's private."

This shark has spent his life swimming against the tide – whatever the cost, aggressively defending what he feels is right. He has never shied away from speaking his mind. When he suspected Jumbo Ozaki was cheating in a tournament, he confronted him – no matter that it was in Japan where Ozaki is thought of as a God.

When he thought Mark McCumber should not have repaired a spike mark he told him so – no matter that McCumber hasn't spoken to him since.

"I think our game is really hurting at the moment," he says unexpectedly. "True, Tiger is a phenomenon and is bringing the game to sectors of society who haven't seen it before. But, look at other sports which have put all their eggs in one basket.

> **"If guys are jealous of my helicopter, they should work harder and get their own. I worked my ass off to get it"**

BUSINESS CLASS
Greg Norman, The
'K' Club, Dublin, July 2002:
"People want to know how
much I'm worth. But it's
private."

Look at the NBA [National Basketball Association] who hung their hat on Michael Jordan's hook for a long time and there was no one to pick up the slack.

"Compare that with what was happening 10 years ago when there were a whole handful of us, all about the same age, all from different parts of the world, and all battling it out – players like Nick Faldo and Nick Price, Freddie Couples, Curtis Strange, Seve Ballesteros and Ian Woosnam. That's a much healthier state of affairs.

"Today, sponsors are unwilling to finance tournaments in America unless Tiger Woods is in the field because of TV ratings and so on. It's pretty hard to go to a title sponsor and say 'Give me $6 million – oh, and by the way, Tiger Woods won't be playing'. If Tiger gets pushed and he wins then that's great but I don't like seeing him win by 15 shots. That's not good for the game."

Sharks don't watch golf on television. Too busy playing golf with Presidents and flying his helicopter. (When he went up in a US Air Force jet a few years ago he made a point of telling reporters he didn't throw up the way Tom Cruise had done while filming Top Gun.) But that doesn't stop him having strong opinions about some of Tiger's adversaries.

"When I heard about Phil's [Mickelson] comments after the US Open this year ["This was certainly not a disappointing day today. It was one of the most exciting days that I've had in the game of golf…It's been wonderful"] I thought 'Hang on a minute'. It can't be wonderful if you finish second. You've got to want to cut Tiger's heart out and eat it right there in front of him. You don't see that nowadays with too many of these guys. They don't seem to want to cut Tiger's heart out and eat it."

It was all getting a bit blood-thirsty. Wasn't he mellowing with age? Had some of his teeth lost their edge over the years? Was he now into wearing yellow cardigans and sipping Horlicks?

"I suppose the natural evolution of time, age and maturity does that to you. When I was young I felt like I was bullet-proof, whether on the golf course or in life in general. As you grow older and you get a wife and kids, you slow down a little bit. You want to absorb things more and you learn to appreciate things more."

He is looking forward to a time when his kids have finished college and he and Laura can spend more time travelling together, perhaps in the new boat he has had built for himself. It is a 228-foot yacht which combines ocean-expedition toughness with cruise-liner luxury.

WORLD ICON
The Great White Shark hits balls off a Great White Shark at the 2000 Sydney Olympics.

Norman on...

THE US PGA TOUR ADMINISTRATION
"It is a quagmire. My surgery enabled me to take a look at the game from outside and when I looked back in, as a businessman, I saw some ugly things. They expect a lot out of you and you feel like you just pass through the organisation. Steve Elkington suggested to Tim Finchem (tour commissioner) at this year's annual dinner at Sawgrass that I become a Board member. That's obviously not going to happen but Steve recognised that with my experience as a player and in business I could be a great asset."

GOLF COURSE DESIGN
"I have a tremendous passion for it. I begin with the end in mind. After getting input from the owner I picture in my mind what we are going to do. And then I go and paint this picture. You've got to be flexible and let things evolve. I'm very meticulous with my projects and probably spend more time on them than other designers."

NICK FALDO
"I was not intimidated by anyone on the golf course. I had a tremendous rivalry with Nick and he was one hell of a competitor. He's a tough guy to play golf with because he gets into his own world. Every other guy I've ever played against acknowledged their opponent's play. Faldo was different. He didn't do that. There was no conversation, but we all knew that. But he's changed as he's got older. Get him off a golf course and he's a funny guy. In relaxed atmosphere he's got a damn good sense of humour."

Although he would love to have won more than two majors (he has finished runner-up on eight other occasions) he is adamant that each of his dramatic losses (against Bob Tway, Larry Mize and Nick Faldo to name but three) have changed his life a lot more than winning would have done.

"The mirror has been my sports psychologist for the past 15 years," he says. "Whenever I've been in a tough predicament, I've looked at myself in the mirror and asked some very tough questions eyeball to eyeball. That's the only time you're going to get the real truth – because you certainly can't lie to yourself.

"Sure, I wish I had won five times as many majors as I have. But all those times I didn't win have produced major dividends in my life and my business. After it's all over, you've got to go away and figure out what went wrong. Was it something mechanical? Was it mental? Was it in your heart? Or was it just destiny? You need to be able to take a little ingredient away, learn from it, and turn a negative into a positive. By losing I became a winner."

It all sounds a touch religious. "I'm not religious," he says. "But I believe in destiny. I believe if you treat life respectfully, it will look after you. I'm a fatalist and I do believe that good things happen to good people."

Does it follow, then (baring in mind the various calamities which have overtaken Norman during the final stages of major championships) that bad things happen to bad people?

"Not really, but I do believe if you take care of your life and accept things as they are, it will all balance out in the end. Last night some Russian kids were killed when their aircraft hit a cargo plane. What about them? How can you explain that? It's very difficult. Was it because they were in the wrong place at the wrong time. I don't know the answer.

"How I am alive after some of the things I did while surf-boarding is beyond me. I would get caught up in a bad wave and dragged to the bottom, and then there is a very fine line between surviving it and not surviving it. Until you go to the other side you don't really know the answer to any of this."

So there is another side, is there?

"I'm not a religious person but over a period of time you start to question things. I know I'm being very ambivalent about all this but that's because I haven't really found where I fit in this programme. Laura is a Catholic and we always say a prayer over our meal every night when the four of us are together. That is just something we feel instills a good value system in our children."

Seldom do you see a shark in such philosophical mood. The moment passed. Sharks are ruthless hunters and they can't stay philosophical for too long. If they do, they stop moving, and if they stop moving they die. Norman was off again, scanning the waters around him, working out who he was going to have for lunch.

"I'll never forget the comment Phil Mickelson made about me one time. He said 'Boy, I hope I have as many chances to win major championships as Greg Norman had, because I bet you I'll win more than two'. I sit back now and laugh at that comment with Tony Navarro [Norman's caddie]. These guys grow up seeing you have all these chances, and they think 'Why can't he do it?' Just wait. Time is going to tell. Until you get there and experience it all, it's pretty hard to make a comment prematurely."

The Shark was getting itchy. They are not good at sitting still for too long. He was now looking at the spotlights in the room. They were voice-activated and kept on flashing, designed to protect the valuable original water colours dotted around the walls. He was looking at the lights and the pictures like a shark looks at a piece of red meat, as if he fancied a bit of that, back in his house in Jupiter, Florida.

Laura, his wife, arrives. "They've been trying to photograph me with a halo around my head," Norman tells her, now with a beer in his hand. "And there was I thinking there was one there all along," she laughs.

So how does Norman want to be remembered? He flashes his cold blue eyes, as if he has just been asked how much money he is worth. After a pause he replies: "As the guy who gave it all, and who never shied away from anything. I hope people will remember how high my morals and ethics are. Maybe as someone who created standards which people tried to emulate."

With that he disappears, out into the dangerous world of autograph hunters and hero worshippers. The girl at reception with pink lipstick smiles sweetly as he passes.

Suddenly, he turns in the corridor, teeth flashing. "Hey, just remember. I don't want to be remembered quite yet." And with a final flick of his tail he vanishes.

THE FUTURE
When their kids have finished college, Norman and his wife Laura plan to spend more time travelling the world together.

Norman on...

THAT 1996 MASTERS COLLAPSE
"Ironically, that was a huge positive boost for me. I had never experienced a bigger uplift in my life during what was, in most people's eyes, a huge down time. People who don't know me can't comprehend that. My wife and my family can comprehend it, because they can see the changes in me. It had a dramatic impact on me because by losing I became a winner."

SEPTEMBER 11
"I was on my ranch in Colorado where there are no telephones and no TVs. As a result we didn't find out about it until two days later on the Thursday, when one of our guys went to get some groceries. I wanted to come home immediately but we weren't allowed to fly until the Saturday. I'm an Australian, and very proud of the fact that Australia is the only country that has stood side by side America in every war they have fought. My wife is American, my kids are American and, since 9/11, I have never felt more American."

WINNING ANOTHER MAJOR
"I still think I can. I watch videos of my swing in 1986 (when Norman won his first Open), and I thought I had a tremendous swing back then. Your mind sees it but your body won't let you get there. But I am trying and I am fitter now than I have been in years and I think I can compete with these young kids."

NICK FALDO

GOLF WORLD   As originally published July 2002

Nick Faldo
KING OF
BRITISH GOLF

He has won two Opens at Muirfield, a third at St Andrews, three Masters green jackets, and is Europe's highest points scorer in the Ryder Cup. Be upstanding for the finest golfer these islands have ever produced.

WORDS: JOCK HOWARD   **MAIN PHOTOGRAPHY:** JAMES CHEADLE

Glory Days...

NICK AND HIS DAD, GEORGE, ARE EXHAUSTED. They have just spent nine hours driving in the car. Despite this, Nick's heart is beating fast. This is 1973, his first experience of the Open Championship, and he can't wait to get out on to the golf course. On the outskirts of Troon, his father pulls his white VW Beetle up at a petrol station, and Nick immediately spots two golfers he recognises.

"It was Tony Jacklin and Tom Weiskopf," says Faldo, "and both of them were wearing their Paddington Bear check trousers. Tony was in his roller, filling up. I turned to my Dad and whispered: 'Wow, look at them?' That got us both really excited."

Father and son stayed in a camp site close to the course. It was so cold and damp that every day Nick wore his pyjamas under his trousers. He was a week away from his 16th birthday. From dawn until dusk he skampered around the dunes like a hare, never setting eyes on his father until the evenings. He tried to watch every shot, running back to the tee to see their drives, darting over the hills to see their second shots, and sprinting to the green to see them putt.

If a puppy had just been shown how to retrieve a stick for the first time, it would not have been more content.

"On the first day I went straight to the practice ground," he says, "and I saw Tom Weiskopf practising in his street shoes. He was pinging these irons away and he had slippery soles on. I thought 'That's impressive, he's going to win'; and I was right.

"A year later, I went to Lytham, ran out onto the course, and the first shot I saw was Gary Player hitting a 3-iron to a foot on the 3rd. I said to my Dad, 'He's going to win'; and he did. (I told Gary that story at Augusta earlier this year, and he came over all dewy-eyed and said 'I don't believe it, man'.)"

You don't have to be clairvoyant to know that the Open Championship has a very prized position in Nick Faldo's heart. He loves going to Augusta every April (where, like the Open, he has been victorious three times) but it will never quite be the same as his own national championship. He has teed it up in every Open since 1975, when he failed to qualify as an 18-year-old amateur. Last year, he missed the cut at Royal Lytham, only the second time in his professional career that he has failed to qualify for the weekend. In his 26 Opens as a professional, as well as three victories in six years, he has finished in the top-10 on no fewer than 12 occasions.

"There is something very special about the Open," he says wistfully. "It is completely different from every other tournament we play. It's the little seaside towns. It's the courses. And it's the galleries which make it so unique. Where else do the crowd applaud the 7 o'clock tee time onto the 1st green? Even the sound of the Open is different. They always have those metal railings, so there's a different ring when you hit the ball."

The Faldo home is a plush house near Runnymede in Berkshire. It is a big, family residence which is over 250 years old. In the considerable garden, there is a row of big, golf umbrellas stuck into the lawn at five-yard intervals, with a few golf balls scattered around them; testimony to an impromptu chipping session Nick had engaged in with his 13-year-old son, Matthew, a few days earlier. Inside the house itself, there is nothing to suggest this man is a golfer, let alone Britain's best ever golfer.

Typical of Faldo to remember the noise at the Open is slightly different than at the other majors, because of the metal railings. His attention to detail is disarming; always has been. When he was younger he used to spend hours cutting his finger nails, to get them just as he wanted, because he was convinced this gave him better feel when he was gripping the club.

Discussing his two victories at Muirfield in 1987 and 1992, his memory for minutiae is astonishing. He is the sort of guy who could tell you what colour socks Rodger Davis was wearing in the third round of the 1987 Open, or the direction of the wind to within five degrees, when he came to the 15th hole in the fourth round in 1992.

"I was trying to make birdies in that last round in 1987," he says. "Everyone makes a big thing of the 18 straight pars, and it used to irritate me a bit when people said I was boring because I churned out all those pars. If it had been four bogeys and four birdies, they would have described it as extraordinarily exciting. I was trying to birdie every hole, but I was nervous. I hadn't won a major before, the weather was like pea soup all week, and I wasn't putting great."

Faldo kicks his trainers off, and rests his socks on the coffee table. As he stretches back on his white, billowy sofa, hands behind his head, you can't help coming to the conclusion that for the first time in years, he is genuinely at peace with himself. Next door in the kitchen, his wife of nearly a year, Valerie, is cooking pasta.

"My second win at Muirfield was very different," he says. "By then I had won four majors, and going into the week I was playing really well. I had terrific inner-confidence and I really felt I could do anything. I was in full control. If I wanted to fade it five yards, or draw it ten yards, or hit it with a slightly higher trajectory, or keep it a wee bit lower, under the wind, I could do it. And then I was holing the putts to boot."

At his best, in the late Eighties and early Nineties, Faldo seemed to many of his fellow professionals to be invincible. His name on a leaderboard had the same effect as Tiger's does now. It caused hardened, skilful men to forget their lines and to start jabbing at two-footers. Scott Hoch and John Cook still have nightmares about Nicholas Alexander Faldo MBE.

"It amuses me when fellow professionals say 'Faldo was lucky because he was given a couple of majors'," he says. "I mean how many do you think Jack [Nicklaus] won because he was in the right place at the right time, when someone else couldn't handle it. That's not being given it. Everyone has their own pressure threshold. Some people can't handle it on the 1st tee; others crack after 71 holes. That's all part of the test." It's a test Faldo past on six occasions with flying colours: that's three Open Championships and three Masters.

TROPHY HUNTER
Showing of his replica Ryder Cup, Masters trophy and Open Championship Claret Jug.

CHEZ FALDO
Nick's back garden, Runnymede, Berkshire, May 14, 2002.

"There is something special about the Open. It's the little seaside towns, the courses, the galleries. Even the sounds are different"

NICK FALDO, CHAMPION AT MUIRFIELD 1987 AND 1992

Love & Hate...

NICK IS UPSTAIRS TAKING A SHOWER. HE has spent the day fishing on the River Test. News reaches us that he has "caught quite a few"; so things are looking up as far as our proposed interview goes. Hopefully, the fact he has caught fish means he will be in a good mood.

Sitting in the Faldo's delightful kitchen (primrose yellow with wedgewood blue work-stations), there is a huge, dark blue Aga at one end. Right in the middle of the room is a goldfish bowl twice the size of a football. Natalie, Nick's 16-year-old daughter, keeps her three fish – Gucci, Pucci, and Piranha – in here. Nick, showing he hasn't lost dead aim, won them at a local fair.

Sitting opposite is Nick's wife, Valerie. She is vivacious, bubbly and full of life. She is also petite, blond and pretty.

"I was wandering Valerie, if it would be at all possible to do a short interview with you?"

"Sure. No problem at all. Now?"

"That would be great. But should we ask if Nick is all right about that? I mean, I don't want him to come downstairs and hit me."

"Oh, he'll be fine," she says laughing. "Don't worry about him."

She looks up the stairs and shouts "You'd better be nice to me or I'm going to say some nasty things."

There were times, in the not-too-distant past, when taking such liberties with the six-time major champion, might well have ended in the accident and emergency ward. His relationship with the British press has been notoriously fractious. In his 26 years as a professional, he has never been totally comfortable with the fact that just because he is a bloody good golfer he should be treated like one of Natalie's goldfish. An intensely shy man by nature, he has found it intolerable that the world and his brother think they have some sort of right to watch his every move. Until now, that is.

HOME COMFORTS
"Isn't there anything else on telly apart from golf, luv?"

"The press has changed in two senses," he says. "Literally, they have changed, in the sense that a lot of them are no longer around. But also, their brief has changed. Editors are much more interested in lifestyle issues nowadays."

Faldo is much more at ease with the press these days. Where previously he was prickly and irritable he is now relaxed and eloquent. Built on sand, and with misunderstanding on both sides, the relationship he shared with the British media more often than not ended in tears. Faldo admits that he has made mistakes in his time; but he also still feels he has been treated harshly.

"I used to invite a writer back to the house like this, and we'd chat away for an hour or so; and then 30 seconds from the end, I'd let my guard down, and say something which I thought was pretty trivial. The next day I'd find the whole story was based on those 30 seconds. That would make my blood boil.

Faldo on 1987

66 When I won the Spanish Open in May, I decided then to focus on winning the Open. All week the weather was like pea soup and it was just a matter of grinding it out. I had a good feeling. Coming down the stretch I was a shot behind Paul Azinger, who was playing in the group behind me. At the 16th, I had 182 yards, and I hit a 2-iron. Then at the 17th, I had to make a decision about whether or not to try to carry the cross bunkers. In the end I decided not to and hit a driver, 5-iron short, and then a 5-iron to the green, and made par. And then on the last, I was just thinking: make a par up the last and you'll win the Open. My approach was a gentle 4-iron shot, but I didn't fancy that, so I threw myself at a 5-iron instead. I was unlucky because it landed on an upslope 40 feet short of the flag and stopped. My first putt was a 'wide', and finished five feet away. I looked at the scoreboard and saw Rodger Davis' name. I remember thinking 'I just don't want to be in a playoff. As I stood over the putt I thought 'This to win the Open'. And in it went. After I signed my card, I sat in the R&A caravan, between two televisions, but I couldn't them. My daughter, Natalie, was in there with me, trying to press all the buttons. All I can remember is sitting with my head in my arms and hearing Peter Alliss say: "The next 15 seconds is going to change one of these guy's lives." I listened like hell for the crowd to tell me what had happened. And when I heard the groan, I knew I had won. 99

"Then, I'd see the writer the next week and he'd say 'So, talk me through your 67. I'd think 'Why do I want to talk to you at all?' 'You stitched me up last week'."

Faldo decided the only thing to do was to close his doors to the press, and he moved to America in 1995, partly to escape from their attentions.

"In the end, though, closing my doors didn't work either," he says, "because they always got the last word. If I closed my doors, I got a reputation for being aloof and unfriendly. And if I opened them, I got screwed. So I couldn't win. I could never handle that. My Dad used to say that even with lousy stories, at least you were making headlines. But, I was too much of an elephant, I guess. I found it difficult to forget."

When he was going through his much publicised divorce from Gill, the paparazzi were out in force, leaping over cars, trying to dig up the dirt. Faldo found himself more often on the front page of the newspapers than on the back; and his children suffered at school because of all the attention.

Ironically, the relationship between Faldo and the British media reached an all-time low when he was reaching his peak, after his Open victory at Muirfield in 1992. In his champion's speech, and in front of millions of people, he thanked the press "from the heart of my bottom".

"I was cheesed off," he says. "I'd been reading so much criticism about me, for such a long time and I just decided, on the spur of the moment, to have a dig back. It was quite interesting because some people thought what I did was dreadful, and others thought it was great. Last week a journalist asked me why I didn't take half a dozen of them aside rather than do it in front of everyone. I said 'When you have a dig at me, and call me an "obnoxious so and so" in your newspaper, you don't take me aside and have a dig. You do it in front of hundreds of thousands of readers'."

FLYING THE FLAG
Britain's finest golfer for 100 years.

Faldo on 1992

❝ I shot 66, 64 in the first two rounds; which is still a record score for 36 holes. By Sunday, I was four shots in the lead. It was mine to lose, really. Slowly, shots began to dwindle away. I started to make mistakes. I hit a bad wedge into the bunker at the 11th and made a 5. And I three-putted the 13th. But, the weird thing was I kept on saying to Fanny I'm all right'. And then I blocked it right on the 14th and I thought 'I don't believe this, I've just thrown it away'. At that moment, I looked at the leaderboard and saw I was two behind John Cook. I hit a half 5-iron into 15. The wind was fractionally left to right, which made it awkward, because I couldn't aim at the pin. I had to aim to land it right on top of the hog's back; knowing that if I pulled it a touch, it would have ended up going left. And it fed right down to three foot from the hole.

On the 16th, I made a really good little up and down from the back of the green. The one that never gets talked about, but for me was crucial, was the 17th. I hit a great drive. Standing on the tee I saw a red post office box in the tented village, and hit a draw off that – and nailed it. That left me with a 4-iron to the green, and that birdie was pivotal. The walk back to the 18th tee was a killer. It's about 80 yards back there, and all the time I was thinking 'Four to win the Open'; because I had just heard the groan from the 18th green, which I knew was Cook making a 5. My 3-iron to the 18th was a great shot, and as I was striding towards the green, Fanny said: "You're leading by one." I'm trying to stay focused, looking ahead, and I say through gritted teeth 'I know'. She's thinking 'How does he know. He hasn't looked at a board'. But I could sense what was happening just from the noise of the crowd. I knew I was leading. ❞

Meet Mrs Faldo

Where did you first meet Nick?
By a salad bar at the Swiss Open.

What three words best describe his character?
Shy, romantic, perfectionist.

What were you doing before you met?
I had just finished a degree in social sciences. My life has totally changed. My family and friends are just amazed at our schedule. I try to keep in touch with friends through the email but it is tricky.

Apart from the goldfish, what pets have you got?
Two Persian cats called Lola and Victor. Actually, Victor's half Persian and half Ginger. One day, we both want to have dogs, cats, cows, horses, the whole lot. This place is going to look like a zoo.

What's your golf like?
Terrible. I am going to get better though. Nick gave me a lesson once at the Faldo Institute in Florida. There were loads of people watching and I couldn't hit the thing at all. It made me mad.

Name Nick's most annoying habit.
Um. That's a difficult one. It's not really annoying, but I guess his biggest fault is he is quite forgetful. He can leave the house three times without taking his mobile. Amazing.

Do you ever talk about the past?
Quite a lot, actually. Over the years he has kept so much back emotionally. I hope I can help him talk about some of that. I come from a family where we talk constantly and openly about everything.

What is he like in the kitchen?
He makes a terrific Spag Bol; although some of that may be to do with Natalie helping him.

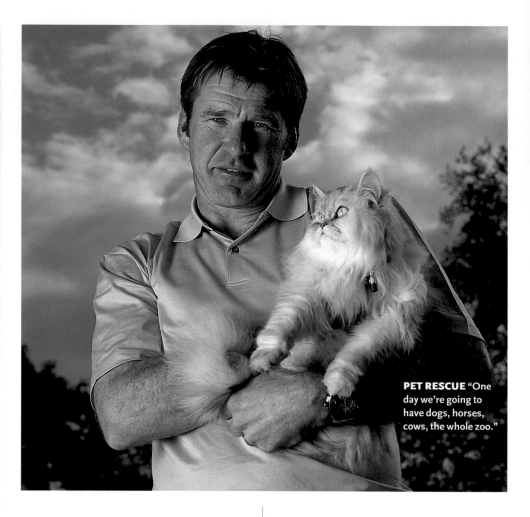

PET RESCUE "One day we're going to have dogs, horses, cows, the whole zoo."

"In his prime, Faldo thought he was immortal," says one of his early biographers, John Hopkins, Chairman of the British Association of Golf Writers and golf correspondent of The Times. "He thought he could fly close to the sun like Icarus, and his wax wouldn't melt. I think he now realises he is mortal. Of course, I have no doubt disgraceful things went on. Unlike in America, where there are perhaps only three national newspapers, we have 15; so the intensity is much greater. He was under enormous scrutiny because the British public have an insatiable appetite to know everything about their superstars, right down to what they have in their dustbins, and Faldo found that incredibly annoying."

Any PR floozy will tell you that if you want to use the press to suit your own ends, you must play their game. It strikes me that this is the one game Faldo has not been very good at over the years. Too often,

the press has floated a fly over his nose, and he has risen at it, leaping out of the water, just like one of those brownies he is so good at catching on the Test.

Perhaps he should have watched how Seve Ballesteros handled the press and was able to use them for his own ends. Maybe now he had learned some lessons.

"Of course I have," he says. "The biggest mistake I made was when a journalist would say a line, and because I didn't disagree with it, it became my quote. That was tough to take, and that's caught me out a few times. But my philosophy in life is to be as nice to as many people as possible along the way, but if someone really makes you mad and pisses you off you might as well tell them. If I do something totally crass and stupid, fine. But what used to infuriate me was when they would just make up stories."

WHERE'S THE COOKER?
"Nick makes a terrific Spag Bol – although he does need help!"

"Life is a bit like golf. You get one shot and if you make a mess of it, you take a seven and walk to the next hole"

Future Plans...

NICK IS HOLDING A UNION JACK FLAG, waiting patiently for the wind to blow. In about 12 hours he flies to Germany to play in the SAP Deutsche Bank Open. It is late. We have over-run on our time. He is hungry and tired, and wants to start packing.

"Next, you're going to ask me put on my Austin Powers shorts and my Blackpool Kiss-me-Quick hat," he says with a big grin.

Valerie arrives, glittering like a butterfly, in brilliant colours. She licks her fingers and presses Nick's hair down. "Isn't that horrible," she says. "That's what my Granny used to do." Faldo grins again.

Nick Faldo has come a long way from the grumpy, selfish, one-dimensional, automaton he was so often portrayed as. His house is elegantly decorated in bright and cheerful colours. There are pictures of sunflowers on the walls. As Loyd Grossman would say: "This would seem to be the house of someone who has found true happiness."

"Valerie has added to the whole picture," says Nick. "She hasn't come on board as a golfing wife. She doesn't always come to tournaments, and if she does, she doesn't walk round and watch me play. I find that really refreshing now. Why would a wife come to their husband's work? The de-briefing at the end of my rounds doesn't last more than a couple of minutes; and then we get on with the rest of our lives."

Faldo still enjoys celebrity status; always has, always will. He lives next door to Elton John and gets invited to parties by Posh and Becks. Even though, by his own admission, his playing days are numbered (he will be 45 on the Thursday of this year's Open) he still spends 45 minutes every day working out, and there is no sign of a receding hairline or expanding waste.

"When Nick arrives on a practice ground," says Tony Johnstone, a tour veteran of 23 years, "you can still hear the buzz go round. Every player out there really respects what he has achieved. He's done what the rest of us have been striving to do – win majors – and he's done it six times. That puts him in a different league from everyone else."

Faldo is at a transitional stage in his career. He is carefully balancing playing, with developing the business side of his career. The Faldo empire off the course is growing fast. He has publicly said he wants to be the next Ryder Cup captain, after Sam Torrance. More and more of his time is now spent growing the 'Faldo' brand, cultivating juniors with his ever-expanding Faldo Junior Series, and designing top quality golf courses. There are now Faldo courses as far apart as Canada and China; and those who know him won't be surprised to hear that every one of them has received rave reviews.

"I don't know any other designer of golf courses," says John Hopkins, "who takes the trouble to go around with a video camera to other famous courses, just to get a better feel for great design. When he played a European tour event in Australia last year, he took time off to go and have a look at Royal Melbourne. That is the attention to detail of the man."

Ask Faldo if he is less of a perfectionist now than he was ten years ago, and he smiles. "Probably. The biggest difference is I'm driven by different things now. In the glory days I always believed I could work at my game and make it a little bit better. I'm a totally different golfer now. I haven't won for five years. I'm out there because I'm enjoying it. I'm also much easier on myself now. If it goes good out on the course, it goes good. If it doesn't, there are other areas of my life, which might have done well."

Ask him if he can win another major and make it a magnificent seven and there is a twinkle in his eye. "The great thing about golf is that you just don't know. Plenty of players have won majors after you didn't think they could. Look at Ben Crenshaw and Jack Nicklaus. That's what we all love about this game. If you get inspired and it suddenly all clicks..."

It is time to leave; but just as he opens the door, the subject of regrets pops up.

"There are lots of things I would have done differently in my life," he says, "given the chance to change things. But, that's what it's all about. There's no rehearsal. If the time comes when I can't hit my hat, then I'd love to be regarded as one of the greatest golf course designers ever. Life is a bit like golf really. You get one shot at it. And if you make a mess, you take a seven, and you walk on to the next hole."

Lola, Faldo's cat, was now giving me the sort of threatening stare his master used to be so good at when your time was up. In that department, at least, Nick Faldo seems to have lost his touch.

41

44 champions' dinners finally take their toll on the King.

WORDS: PAUL MAHONEY
PHOTOGRAPHY: PHIL SHELDON & ALLSPORT

THE NUMBER NEXT TO ARNOLD Palmer's name on the 1st tee was 84. "Is that Arnie's age?" a young American voice asked his pop. Pop wasn't sure. Could be.

Such was the vigour of adoration for Palmer at the Masters, pop was probably only one of many who hadn't bothered to check out their man's playing partners. If they had, they would have realised if Palmer was indeed 84 then, by the same system, his playing partners, Japan's Toru Taniguchi and the USA's amateur championship runner-up Robert Hamilton, had performed rather well to qualify for the season's first and most exclusive major aged just 12 and 15 respectively. The number against their name referred not to their age or score but to the caddie's registration number. Such is the legend of the King, it is easy to buy into the illusion that he is somewhat ageless, like all decent gods worth their salt. The very latest junior recruits to Arnie's Army could perhaps be forgiven for thinking this. But there are clearly some more seasoned campaigners sporting very large rose-tinted spectacles who believe their Mr Palmer will live forever.

Arnie's last stand

Jack pulled out with a dicky back, Gary plodded on regardless and Arnie took just one hole to decide it was time to finally break up the Old Big 3. Golf World joined the galleries at the Masters to witness the end of the Nicklaus, Player and Palmer era.

Arnie's first tee shot was a 3-wood. "I hit that sonofabitch as hard as I could," he roared – but it still didn't make it to the bunkers at the top of the hill. His 40-foot putt at the 1st sped up to the flag from the bottom of the slope, the brakes failed, and his ball kept on rolling, sliding down the hill and off the bottom of the green. Arnie grimaced and his Army groaned. He four-putted and admitted later this was the moment he knew "the writing was on the wall".

As he walked to the 2nd tee he winked at a lady he recognised – Arnie always has an eye for the ladies – and stopped briefly to say hello to a few familiar faces in the front row. "Go Arnie!" yelled a well-meaning fan. It must be assumed it was an encouragement rather than a suggestion that he go and put his feet up. But it did feel rather ill-timed, especially as that would indeed prove to be the moment when Arnie decided to 'Go'.

It is 44 years since Palmer won his first major at the Masters and 40 years since the Old Big 3 of Jack Nicklaus, Gary Player and Palmer bagged a clean sweep of the majors in one season, four years even before England would win the World Cup. And here they all were still turning up at Augusta in the second week of April. Except this would be the end of the line for this Great Triumvirate. It would stop a run of 48 consecutive Masters for Palmer. Jack Nicklaus pitched up at the beginning of the week for the champions' dinner and presumably to be adored just a little bit more. He would be missing just his second ever Masters since 1959. He pulled out of the tournament saying "my back is in a mess." It no doubt is but then Jack also said he had played the course a few weeks before the Masters and shot 76, 81. "I was hitting 3-woods and 4-woods into some greens," he shrugged. "I don't want to display what I've got out there," he said understandably but sadly. "I play golf like I ski and play tennis now," he half-laughed. It doesn't look like he will ever tee it up in a major again. That shouldn't really be surprising – he is 62 years old.

Gary Player still soldiers on alone even though he trudged to a rather anonymous 80, 78 before sloping off home. As the fittest of this celebrated trio, aged a sprightly 66, he also can see his days are numbered. He's been drumming up support for a Golden Oldies tournament during Masters week – an OAPs (Over-Achieving Pros) Masters, if you like. But Palmer doesn't fancy the idea while Nicklaus thought it could be fun but dismissed it saying: "This is the greatest tournament in the world. Why would you want to clutter it up with a bunch of old guys?"

Palmer's front nine in his penultimate round was a disastrous 48 hacks, pulled hooks, multiple putts, topped drives and duffed chips. Yet he chatted, waved, smiled and gave that old fashioned thumbs up to His People all the way to an 89. "Tomorrow will be it," he announced, eyes glazing over behind the 18th green. "I was short and crooked today," he joked. He was referring to his game but the thought did occur that it is precisely how he looks and moves these days. The twinkle in his eyes is still there along with the charming grin. So is his Tintin quiff – albeit grey and tired rather than the sexy greased back jet black cool of yesteryear. His perma-tan neck and face now stretch out of the top of his polo shirt like a sun-dried tortoise peaking out of its shell.

"I hope I won't embarrass myself," he added humbly before leaving in his white cadillac. To save any such embarrassment during his final round, the scoreboard monitors, presumably fully kitted out members of his Army, removed his total score (which would finish at 30-over for those who want the gory details) from the leaderboards around the course. It made a statement that this wasn't about shooting the lights out. The man is 72, for goodness sake. Either that or they were having trouble totting up his double bogies. No, this would be one last procession for the King: a 2002 reunion of all those Palmer love-ins from his glory days in the Swinging Sixties.

Jack would regret choosing the golf cart coupé.

I've never enjoyed just making a cut. I might not be competitive enough to win…but I'm not going out there hitting 3 and 4-woods

It is appropriate the scoreboard monitors made such a symbolic gesture of support and affection. It was back in 1958 when the flamboyant and charismatic Palmer was storming through the field to his first of four green jackets that his legend was born. "The scoreboards in those days were manned by soldiers from the local Fort Gordon Army Base," explains Palmer's long-time friend and business partner Doc Giffin. "They adopted Arnie and posted signs on the boards proclaiming themselves to be Arnie's Army. And it stuck." "People started carrying signs and holding up banners," Palmer said, "and it got pretty heavy! Not just at Augusta but all over the world. Then I think they banned people from carrying signs," he smiled.

Arnie's Army had packed themselves 10-deep around the 1st tee on Friday to witness his final drive in front of the famous clubhouse. At one minute to 1pm they chanted: "Arnie! Arnie!" as he tottered across from the practice putting green. People gawped wide-eyed and grinned endlessly at Arnie who was whistling nervously to himself.

King Arnold I is the nearest thing America has had to Royalty and it felt like those occasions where hundreds of thousands of barmy loyal subjects camp out all night to wave at the Queen and swear blindly that she caught their eye as she passed along the

Mall. Arnie nailed his 3-wood – short again. And off went his Royal procession, receiving standing ovations on every green. Palmer spent every hole walking beside the spectator ropes. Mostly to be close to His People but also because that's mostly where his shots landed.

As Palmer reached the 13th tee of Amen Corner in the heart of his kingdom, the brooding clouds opened up and the heaven's lashed down on poor Arnie and drenched his Army. It was as if even the angels were weeping – gosh you see how easy it is to see symbolism in everything on such emotional days. Heck it just belted down at 4.50pm and play was abondoned. Amen to all that, then. But far from being disappointed, this allowed Arnie one last hurrah and prolonged his long goodbye. "I was very excited," he grinned on Friday evening, "because I haven't played on Saturday for a long time!" Palmer hadn't made the cut since 1983.

You could hear and feel the Mexican wave of emotion following Palmer up the 18th green long before he ambled around the dogleg. A drive and a 3-wood still left him 50 yards short of the green. His Army was 70-deep around the green and they were a whoopin' and a hollerin'. For those of us who weren't here when he was winning, this is how it must have been. Many couldn't possibly have seen anything other than the

> 66There comes a time when you are not competitive, you must say thanks for a great time and call it a day99

Counting his shots to the green causes Gary to doze off yet again.

HE'S THE MAN!
WHAT ARNIE'S PEERS THINK OF **THE KING**

66It will be weird not having him and Jack playing. Arnold is the King but sometimes you've just gotta hang up your spikes.99 Tiger Woods

66Think the Masters and you think Jack and Arnie and Gary.99 David Duval

66I love the guy. When Arnold comes out of the clubhouse, everyone pays attention to him. His scores are irrelevant.99 Fred Couples

66I have the utmost respect for Arnold and all he has done. He is a wonderful player and person.99 Seve Ballesteros

66He made the Masters what it is today and became a matinee idol. We are all going to miss him.99 Tom Watson

66Arnold deserves all the adulation he gets.99 Gary Player

66A great model for all of us. He made golf what it is now. I look up to him as a golfer and a person.99 Bernhard Langer

66He was always like a brother figure to me. I stopped to watch him out there.99 John Daly

66Every player from Charles Howell and Tiger Woods to the old guys like me should take their hat off to Arnold. The way golf is today is all down to him.99 Greg Norman

66I got him to autograph my hat. This was a great moment in my life. I had goose bumps out there. Everybody loves him.99 Final round playing partner Robert Hamilton

66Arnold just loves to play golf and people love him.99 Jack Nicklaus

neck of the person in front. But just being there seemed important. "They are wonderful people," Palmer said after his round, taking a moment to choke back the tears. "I've been out here so long, the galleries are either relatives or we're on first name terms!"

At 10.46am Arnie bent over his final putt, his little pot belly inside his sweaty pink polo shirt bulging over his belt. The final statistic dropped on his 147th 18th green at the Masters in 48 years. He didn't even bother to remove his glove. He just tapped it, took a bow, waved goodbye and was gone. There was no curtain call; Friday's retirement rain-check had given him his Saturday morning encore.

So the heirs to Palmer, Nicklaus and Player are Woods, Mickelson and Duval with perhaps Els carrying the torch for his compatriot Player. Woods, as the kingpin, has quite some way to go to even match the impact Palmer has had on golf, despite the boastings of his rather too confident father Earl. "I played a practice round in 1995 with Jack and Arnie when I was a 19-year-old kid," Tiger said at the Masters. "I didn't know *anything*. I remember Arnie birdied the 18th to win all the skins." Woods again joined Arnie for the traditional pre-tournament Par-3 larkabout contest.

"There will come a point in time where it will be neat to tell my grandkids that 'Hey, I played with the great Arnold Palmer in his last Masters – even it was just in the Par-3 competition!"

Then Tiger got all serious. "Arnie has told me to be an ambassador," he said. The King has finally abdicated and his crown has clearly been officially handed over.

Golfing Greats

SEVE BALLESTEROS

As originally published March 2002

H is dazzlingly whiter than white teeth are the first things you notice. An oblong of gleaming neon in the middle of his face, accentuated further by his caramel-coloured Spanish skin, stretched and toasted over the years by too many hours thrashing golf balls in the midday sun.

Seve is all smiles – flashing those blindingly shiny trademark molars that today cause housewives to swoon and once made teenage girls scream and tear after him because he was prettier than their pop idols. The thick, coal black hair now has nature's grey highlights and is thinning. Yet he is still sickeningly handsome.

Seve is all smiles because we are taking pictures. Try grinning in front of a mirror for 30 minutes and see how hideous you begin to look when the novelty wears off. See how your grins become more like gurns. But the camera loves Seve. His deep-set brown eyes sparkle at the sight of a lens and those perfect teeth form perfect smiles, wrinkling his face in just the right places. He smiles as naturally as leaves fall from trees. Every time he grins it's like a flash bulb exploding in his mouth.

Seve has been performing this routine for 30 years. He's brilliant at

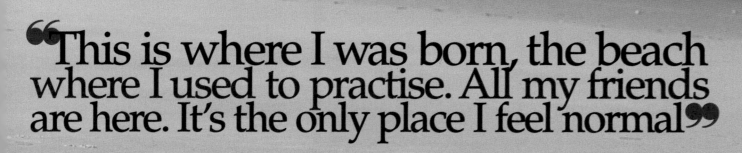

> **"This is where I was born, the beach where I used to practise. All my friends are here. It's the only place I feel normal"**

it. And bored. Hates it. Doesn't even like talking about himself. Doesn't enjoy sitting at a table when all that people around him can do is fawn over him and tell him how fantastic he is. He admits this not as a complaint at having to pose and smile yet again and bear his soul but merely as a statement of fact. It's part of his job.

Despite this, he is charming, co-operative and seems relaxed. And so he should be. We are in Pedrena, stuck on a peninsula between Bilbao and Santander in north eastern Spain. This is Seve's home village (population just 1,500), where he was born, went to school, learned to play golf with a 3-iron on the beach and where he still lives today overlooking the course with wife Carmen and their three children.

It is a measure of his self-confidence – at least on the outside – that he is able to smile at all these days for his golf is no laughing matter. He hasn't won since, fittingly,

the Spanish Open in 1995 and is making less prime cuts than a butcher in a village full of vegans. He's won three Open Championships, two Masters green jackets, beaten the Americans in the Ryder Cup as a player and captain, and been World No.1. A recent poll of European club golfers voted him more popular than Tiger Woods, Nick Faldo and Jack Nicklaus, so why on earth does he bother to travel around the globe shooting 78s and missing cuts on damp Friday afternoons? Ian Baker-Finch, the 1991 Open champion whose magic also deserted him, believes Seve must be going through hell.

Seve pauses for longer than seems natural to find the right words to reply. Finally, he sighs and speaks slower and deeper than he has been. He clearly realises the significance of what he is about to confess. "I am not going through hell," he says softly and unconvincingly. "It is tough when you are used to playing at a certain level and

then all of a sudden you don't play so well." He pauses again, and his shoulders drop. "Ah, it's bad," he winces. He may be smiling on the outside but now you can tell on the inside he is hurting.

"But I have had a wonderful career and I have a wonderful life. I don't have to cry or complain. I'm healthy, have a great family and enjoy a good lifestyle. Through life there are always difficulties. Every day something goes wrong that you don't like but that is how it is." It feels very much like Seve is going through hell. But he perhaps feels that to admit it would be a sign of weakness, an admission of defeat.

Seve is frank about the fact that it is his wayward driving and the subsequent loss of confidence that has seen him plummet to the foot of the European rankings. But he is probably the only person in golf who still truly believes he can win again.

Seve is in denial. Like an alcoholic who stubbornly believes he can solve his own addiction and that no-one else understands what he is going through, Seve too is perhaps too proud to know when to call it a day.

But he is not alone. We mere mortals get told when we can no longer cut the mustard. They call it retirement. They pat us on the head, hand us a carriage clock with which to watch the rest of our lives tick by and wave us goodbye. For most, it's a blessed relief. But what if you have spent your life in the public eye, being idolised, making your dreams come true, fighting like gladiators and reaping untold gold and trinkets. It's tougher to walk away. "Golf is my life," Seve admits. "What can I do? Go home and watch TV? Drive the kids to school? There is always tomorrow. I will never give in."

There is genuine fear that once those who have achieved greatness hold up their hands, part of them dies. Sporting heroes are condemned to die twice – and they all know it. The world had to watch as Muhammad Ali endured one fight too many. Jack Nicklaus cuts a sorry figure now refusing to acknowledge the sands of time. Arnold Palmer is already an embarrassing circus act. No one wants to remember their hero stumbling to treble bogies. Seve's fans still turn up to worship him in their droves (his match against Sam Torrance in the World Matchplay at Wentworth last October drew the biggest galleries) but these days they come more in hope than expectation. People love him because he plays golf like the rest of us – but he can conjure up recovery shots we can only dream about.

Talk of this leads Seve to insist he can still win. "See what Bernhard Langer has done – and Ian Woosnam. For half of last season he was saying he was going to retire, then he nearly won the Open and did win the Matchplay. Des Smyth won aged 49," he emphasises. "And Jack and Hale Irwin won in their Forties, too. To dream and to have hope doesn't cost anything." This all feels and sounds rather desperate.

"I love to compete," he says. And that's the problem with Jack and Seve and why Ali fought on and why Michael Jordan is back playing a young man's game aged 39. That's what they do, that's what made them great, they know nothing else. That's why the Seniors Tour is a glamorous opportunity to renew old rivalries. And it sure beats a carriage clock. "I'm not sure now, but maybe I will decide to play on the Seniors Tour," he admits. "That

would be some tour, wouldn't it? Me and Nick Faldo, Bernhard Langer, Sandy Lyle, Woosie. It will be like starting again."

Where Seve started playing was on his beloved beach, digging a hole with his 3-iron and making a flag stick out of a twig and a piece of paper. He was happy to recreate the old days for the photographs, even adopting that matador stance from the Open at St Andrews in 1984. "It became my trademark," he says proudly.

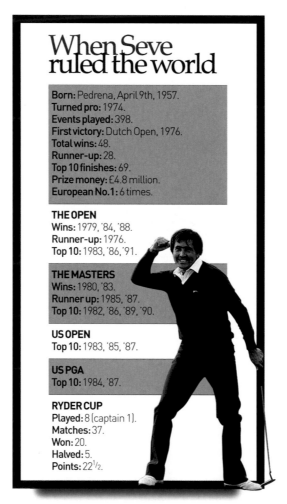

When Seve ruled the world

Born: Pedrena, April 9th, 1957.
Turned pro: 1974.
Events played: 398.
First victory: Dutch Open, 1976.
Total wins: 48.
Runner-up: 28.
Top 10 finishes: 69.
Prize money: £4.8 million.
European No.1: 6 times.

THE OPEN
Wins: 1979, '84, '88.
Runner-up: 1976.
Top 10: 1983, '86, '91.

THE MASTERS
Wins: 1980, '83.
Runner up: 1985, '87.
Top 10: 1982, '86, '89, '90.

US OPEN
Top 10: 1983, '85, '87.

US PGA
Top 10: 1984, '87.

RYDER CUP
Played: 8 (captain 1).
Matches: 37.
Won: 20.
Halved: 5.
Points: 22½.

We drove from the clubhouse at Pedrena to the beach in a dusty, battered old Peugeot, a life-long friend of Seve's offering to give us a lift. He chugged past all the empty parking spaces and pulled up, illegally, almost on the sand so we wouldn't have to carry the photographic equipment too far. A police patrol spotted us and an officer shouted

over. Seve got out of the car and waved. The officer waved back, got back in his car and sped off. The local hero can obviously do pretty much what he likes.

Pedrena is a tiny tumbleweed fishing village; Seve is the big shot – but not the big head. Many of his childhood friends still live and work in the area as fishermen, caddies, farmers and factory workers. Although Seve now lives in the Big House he is still the Seve they have always known. "I've watched him grow up," says the manger of the clubhouse at the golf course, "and he is much the same as he ever was. He just has the problem with the driver now," he whispers.

"I don't think I've changed much," Seve says. "I still socialise with everyone, eat in the restaurants, go to the bars. We just talk about golf and football. They don't see me as higher than them. They treat me like they always have. This is my home. People are not jealous. Okay, I have a bigger house because I need it. But I live modestly. I don't have a Ferrari or a jet. I drive the children in a Range Rover because it is big enough and safe. Pedrena is a wealthy village now. Everyone has cars and televisions and a job."

It wasn't always so. When Seve was mostly bunking off school to practise golf or sneaking out to play on the back nine of the golf course in near darkness, life was tough. There was only one television – in the corner of the local bar – and only one car, bought by his uncle, Pedrena golf club's pro, Ramon Sota after he finished sixth at the Masters in 1965.

"Our house seemed quite big: there were two floors. The cows lived in a shed on the first floor and heated the rooms upstairs," Seve explains. "When I made big money, the first thing I did was pay for a new house for everyone. We all lived together. I stayed with my parents until I got married 14 years ago. His mother Carmen still has her home 25 yards from Seve's. "There is heating and a television. She has a washing machine now, too!"

Seve remembers how his father Baldomero had to fish and farm and caddie to make ends meet. "You don't really notice it at the time but I look back and think what they did for us was incredible." As the youngest of four brothers Seve was lumbered with all the dirty jobs like mucking out the cows and polishing everyone's shoes. He also got stuck with their hand-me-down clothes. This close-knit family life with its hard work ethic (Seve's pocket money was five pesetas for completing all his chores and he used to sell his Sunday creme caramel pudding to his brother Vicente to double his money) taught Seve important les-

The beach at Pedrena, aged 19. The old ladies loved fishing for Seve's lost balls.

sons. He learned to survive, fight for what he wanted, stand up for himself, respect his elders and appreciate the importance of a loving family nucleus. He learned to respect money too.

Life changed dramatically when he began to win on tour. It helped, too, that he married the daughter of the richest man in Spain. Yet all this wealth has never gone to his head. "I have always stayed loyal to my roots," he says. Such an attitude is why he is still able to live in Pedrena and why he is a local hero.

But it very nearly didn't happen. The pre-teens Seve wasn't a troublemaker but he and his pals did steal golf balls off tourists. "If they had two dozen balls in their bag, we would take one dozen and hide them in bushes," he admits. "I also used to step on balls in the rough, mark the spot and collect them later."

No-one at the club could prove what he and his pals were up to so they got away with it. "We would set dustbins on fire and steal the flags from the holes. But one incident of high spirits after midnight on New Year's Eve in 1973 changed Seve's life. He and his gang rolled some irrigation pipes 200 metres down the hill at the 6th hole.

"At the start I enjoyed it on tour. But you get tired. It's a weird world"

Officials found out and Seve was suspended from the club. "My uncle new someone who was able to offer me a job in a factory making sailing boats. I didn't want to work there but it nearly happened." Seve instead turned professional in March 1974, aged 16.

He appears much more comfortable reminiscing about the good old days than talking about what the future holds. It's as if deep down he knows his career has almost come full circle. "The Ballesteros era is over," he admits. "But I was the Tiger of my day." Those are not the words of a man who truly believes, despite his protestations, that

he can win a regular tournament again, let alone a major.

"At the beginning I enjoyed it on tour," he says. "It's like when you fly for the first time – everything is fantastic. But you get tired of it. You eat in wonderful restaurants and stay in five-star hotels but it's a weird world. You are not living like a normal person. When I come home, I feel happier. I like to be home. It makes me feel normal.

"When I go to tournaments, everyone shouts my name and idolises me. I feel embarrassed. To be honest, I'm tired of that, I don't like it." These are indeed the words of a man who must surely be thinking of hanging up his spikes. A man who is evidently not content travelling to miss cuts time and time again. He is much happier taking his children to watch Santander play football on Sundays. "There is no-one famous playing for them. Only their mothers would recognise them!" he laughs.

That Seve has kept his feet on the ground can perhaps be attributed to his mother. His stubborn yet optimistic streak he owes to his father. "He always believed in me," Seve says. The British public has always loved him too. "It pushes me, motivates me, keeps me alive," he says. Perhaps when they can no longer share with him the pain of witnessing his diminishing talents, then he will find it easier to stay at home.

Seve says he never really had a plan but used to dream about being the best player and winning the Open and the Masters. "It was always those two – never the US Open or the US PGA. Funny, really!" His dreams came true but they are fading. They are now just grainy video memories to be replayed for his children.

Seve is battling with his head and heart. His head refuses to give up. "Struggling on tour bothers me in that I want to play better. But I am happy and mentally prepared for what is happening to me." But his heart does not seem to be in it any more and it is to home and, especially, his children that he keeps returning. "They don't understand what I am going through. But whether I miss a cut or not, as soon as I walk through the door, I am home. Watching my children grow up is a thrill many parents don't get. I am living in a wonderful village. This is the best place in the world."

Seve again doesn't seem to have a plan but home is where his heart lies. His days on tour are clearly numbered.

WORDS: **PAUL MAHONEY**
PHOTOGRAPHY: **LLOYD ROGERS**

I realise I am already a role model and it is not easy to live with when you are so young. It's hard to be in control of your emotions all the time. I do the best I can

Dozens of hyperactive school children are racing around, whacking oversized plastic golf balls at orange cones and, worryingly, at each other with red, blue and yellow chunky plastic clubs. All are togged out in caps and polo shirts – one adidas freebie size fits all. Except the tall boys look like theirs have shrunk in the wash and the toddlers are modelling smocks. One of them clearly isn't bothered by all this fuss designed to introduce a new generation to the joys of the auld game. He has wandered off to play keepy-uppy with his football – and

doing rather nicely actually. Until he loses control and flicks one out of reach, high into the air to land slap in the middle of a bunker – just as the greenkeeper is standing back to admire the beautiful curly rake pattern he has completed. His shoulders sag and his expression says: "Bloody kids!" He stares over to see which of the little treasures he can yell at for ruining his Tate Modern entry. He starts raking again when he spots the offending little treasure is the 22-year-old fifth best golfer in the world. Sergio Garcia is giggling and apologising at the same time. The kids love him now. He is one of them.

A quick glance at the youngsters assembled on the practice ground at Loch Lomond Golf Club, near Glasgow, last July, and it isn't so easy to spot Garcia among his new school chums. Plus he has rather foolishly positioned himself next to a particularly gangly 11-year-old for the warm-up routine ("clasp your hands around a polystyrene cup of coffee on the 1st tee" is not, you may be surprised to hear, in the PGA training manual).

This Carry On Golfing caper merely emphasises how new all this attention is for Garcia. It is easy to forget this millionaire sporting star has only recently left behind his teenage years. All of which explains why he looks terribly self-conscious and ill at ease.

Sergio doesn't yet have that stand-out-from-the-crowd aura that Nick Faldo, Seve and Tiger have in shovel-loads. And it is not just down to his slight frame, boyish face and Action Man No.1 haircut. Garcia claims to be 5ft 10 inches tall but appears several inches shorter. He certainly knows how to milk his audience when he goes to work at a tournament and he has already developed an instinct to know when the camera is on him. But he is still learning

how best to handle the extra-curricular activities he is required to perform for his sponsors. After a shaky start to this PR stunt, the kids warm to him and scramble for autographs before their latest superhero is whisked away in a buggy.

"I realise I am already a role model and it's not easy to live with when you are so young," Garcia admits, rather maturely. "It's fun, too, though, to know that young kids (remember Garcia is still only 22) are looking up to you, copying you and want to be like you. I try my best and sometimes I do things that people don't like but we are all human and it's hard to be in control of your emotions and do the right thing all the time."

ONE WEEK later, Garcia is snuffling at the base of a bush wondering how to get his errant drive back on to the 6th fairway during the second round of the Open at Royal Lytham. Hordes of spectators have crowded round to watch his crisis up close. You couldn't see him beneath the branches and dense foliage but you sure could hear him. F***! F***! F***! F***! F***! he blurts like a moped running out of gas. The superbrat is back.

Tiger Woods is in similar trouble at the 12th. He covers his mouth with his hand. Not to stifle a hay-fevery cough but to muffle his voice and to ensure amateur lip-readers

Is technology ruining golf? Sergio Garcia tests the R&A's new clubs and balls designed not to fly so far.

watching on TV can't make out his mumbled Anglo Saxon tribute to fornication. He has learned his lesson after being caught swearing on the 18th tee at the AT&T Pebble Beach Pro-Am. Tiger's awareness of the spotlight he is under is more advanced than Sergio's. Understandably so, too. He is three years ahead of Garcia on golf's merry-go-round and is used to the ride.

Sergio has been accused of being a superbrat due to some high profile fall-outs with authority and the occasional eruption of his Latin temperament. Exhibit A: that shoe-kicking tantrum at Wentworth after slipping during his tee shot. Exhibit B: a tongue-lashing for senior tour referee John Paramor who ruled against him. Exhibit C: an on-course barney with a pro-am partner who accused him of giving duff yardage calls. Exhibit D: slating the greens at Loch Lomond. While Woods is now a goody-two shoes, he too had moments to forget in his first few years on tour. An American men's fashion magazine published blue jokes Tiger cracked in the back of a limousine, and he has been chastised for slamming clubs into fairways and for failing to turn up for pro-am dinners.

But both Woods and Garcia have been thrown into a lifestyle where everything is essentially free, where they have five-star treatment, and an entourage to do their donkey work while all they have to do is smile a bit and play golf. They are in their twenties, the roads are indeed paved with gold and everyone tells them how wonderful they are. All the time. How would you behave just out of your teens?

I am stronger now and I think I have matured. I have learned how to handle pressure better and know I just have to stay calm. Hopefully, then, I will reach Tiger's level

GARCIA's confident delivery of traditional Anglo Saxon profanity at the Open (his squeaky voice even has a slight American twang) is testament to what a fast learner he is and how far he has developed. No, really. In the summer of 1999, I spoke with him for the first time at Wentworth just after he had turned professional having finished top amateur at the Masters (the only British Amateur Champion to do so). He was polite and courteous but painfully shy and quietly spoken, hardly daring to look me in the eye. His basic English was fine but questions had to be kept simple and I found myself talk-ing o-ver-ly slow-ly, the way we Brit-ish talk to old people and make our-selves un-der-stood a-broad. Garcia's answers were largely bite-sized polite cliches about doing the best he can and seeing what happens. But

it was an impressive debut, nevertheless, when you consider the best the average 19-year-old Brit can muster in Spanish is: "Dos San Miguel, por favor." Or "Hasta la vista, baby."

WHILE the greenkeeper at Loch Lomond was no doubt nailing the schoolkids to yardage markers on the driving range with an industrial staple gun, a more comfortable, confident, tactile and outspoken Garcia chatted in the posh tent that was doubling as the locker room. Only members are allowed in the real posh clubhouse – it's a power thing. "I have learned a lot through playing more," Garcia says. "The year I didn't win (2000) taught me a lot about how far I had come and how to handle myself under pressure. I am stronger now and I think I have matured. I have learned that I just have to stay calm. I have been concentrating on that much more for the last four months. Hopefully, then, I will reach Tiger's level. But I need to give it time."

Hopefully, he won't calm down completely. Too many pros these days are so in their zones, the PGA is considering employing paramedics on the tees to check for pulse rates and charisma. It seems that to succeed at the top, any trace of emotion must be ironed out – with extra starch in many cases. Even Woods has down-sized his flailing, here-it-comes haymaker of a punch to a slow, deliberate up-yours uppercut that he unveiled at the Open in 2000 and threw again at the Masters last year. Tiger has come a long way since that knockout punch at Augusta in 1997. He doesn't slam chunks out of fairways anymore either. And this character metamorphosis hasn't gone unnoticed by Garcia. "You don't have to be all serious when you are playing badly," he says. "And you don't have to be all happy when things are going well. You have to find the mid-point. Look at Tiger, you don't see his big air punches as much as you used to." So cherish that memory of Garcia's Jonathan Edwards-like hop, skip and jump that followed his eyes-closed 6-iron from the base of a tree 185 yards to the green at the USPGA Championship in 1999. "I was amazed at the reaction that got," he smiles. "I just wanted to see where my ball went," he adds, matter-of-factly like it was perfectly normal behaviour for a tour pro going head to head with Tiger Woods in a major. "That's probably the biggest reaction I have had in my life from the public." Apart from the "Ser-gio! Ser-gio!" chants that accompanied his inaugural pro round 62 at the Byron Nelson Classic in Dallas 1999. That amount of audience participation hadn't happened (Ryder Cups not included) since Tigermania broke out at Royal Lytham in 1997.

Nobody noticed Class 3B's ringer. He's the skinny looking lad eight from the right in the black slacks.

Even for a photograph
holding a plastic club,
Sergio gripped and
re-gripped 35 times until
he felt comfortable.

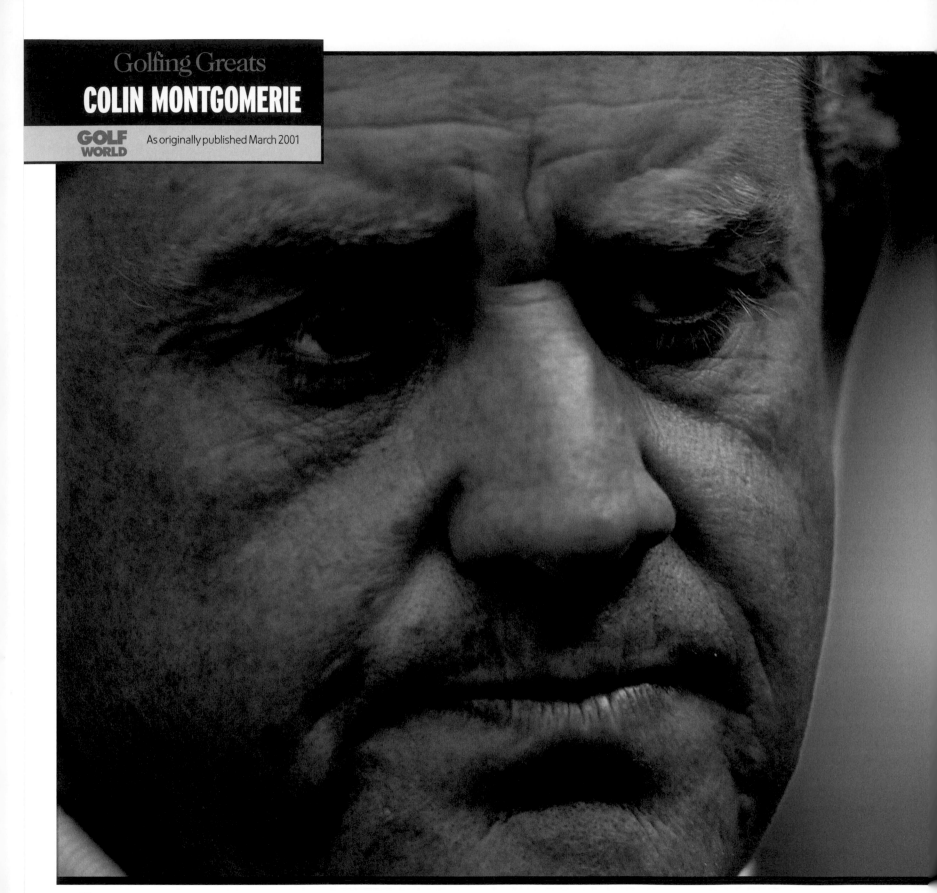

The Trouble with Monty

In the heat of the majors, he has failed to deliver. When something upsets him, he throws a tantrum. At least, that's what Colin Montgomerie's detractors say. So how does he defend himself against charges that he is bad-tempered and past his best? Gary Firkins finds out.

THE CHARGES

THE CASE AGAINST COLIN Montgomerie is gathering pace. According to his critics, Monty's failure to win an eighth consecutive European Order of Merit last season represented a major step backwards in his career. Some believe that, at the age of 37, he won't be coming back.

Not much chance of him winning that elusive major, then. He may have been within a whisker of winning three US Opens and a USPGA in his time, but the fact is he has failed to land a big one.

That's not so surprising, though, because according to his detractors he has failed to master his temper. At the end-of-season Volvo Masters, "moody Monty" was seen by the newspapers "raging" around the course and "venting his anger" on a photographer, a score

recorder, a TV sound girl and assorted members of the crowd.

With such outbursts the Scot has not endeared himself to the press and public. Especially in America, where they soon found some simple name-calling could easily get his goat. 'Mrs Doubtfire', a reference to his appearance, was the nickname he hated most. But that was among the more affectionate jibes he faced during the 1999 Ryder Cup.

Of course, Monty perhaps hasn't helped himself when it comes to public relations. Known not to appreciate being spotted in the street, he likes to hide away with his family. In winter he hibernates for long periods, staying away from the practice range. All to maintain his sanity, he says. It makes some people wonder whether he really enjoys golf at all...

Monty locks horns with Lee Westwood in the World Matchplay final. The outcome foreshadowed the Order of Merit race.

THE INTERVIEW

COLIN MONTGOMERIE is pouring himself a soft drink as I enter the hotel bedroom. He's deep in discussion with someone from his management company and doesn't notice my approach, despite the fact that a public relations person and a photographer come trailing in behind me.

"Oh, I'm sorry," says Monty in a weary voice, finally turning towards me. He looks tired, and for a second I wonder if I've caught him on a bad day.

Corporate events for sponsors are occasions that pro golfers rarely relish, and this weekend Monty is top billing at the Lexus European Cup in Marseilles, an amateur event saturated with glossy new cars. As the face of Lexus, the world number six has a crammed schedule of meetings, clinics and dinners. Probably not the most relaxing way to round off a frustrating year of 'failure', then.

But Monty seems to have succumbed to a little Mediterranean sunshine and turns out

to be in easy-going mood. There's a warm smile as we shake hands. The revised forecast for the interview, I think to myself, is fair rather than gloomy.

After taking the air on a balcony with views across the sumptuous Golf de Frégate, we sit down to talk. Monty's thoughts turn to the year that was – the year he failed to maintain his status as Europe's best.

"I've enjoyed being on top of Europe for so long," he says. "It's been fabulous. But at the same time it's been a great, great strain to stay there, because anyone knows that finishing second is a failure. Like Steve Redgrave at the Olympics. He knew that silver would be seen as failure."

True enough – but suddenly Monty interrupts himself... "Hang on a minute," he says. "Please don't write that the year was a failure – let's write about the seven that were fantastic successes."

That's a fair point too, of course. But it also acknowledges that there's a whisker-fine line

between 'success' and 'failure'. So what did happen last season, I ask?

"I won six times in 1999 and then only twice in 2000, so people think: 'That's not as good as it was.' But I couldn't keep on doing what I was doing. It had to stop – well, slow down sometime. I had 13 years of improving every year. My Order of Merit position never went down. I got to number one and stuck there.

"Last year I just didn't have that run of the

> "I've enjoyed being on top of Europe for so long. It's been fabulous. But at the same time it's been a great, great strain to stay there."

How important has psychology been in Colin winning so much over the past eight years?

For all golfers at that elite, top-50 level, it plays a critical factor because despite all of their differences in technique and everything else, fundamentally there is little difference in the skill levels. What does make the difference is the mental side.

Is there a psychological reason why a player who has dominated the game for a long period might suddenly suffer inconsistent results?

If you've been improving for 13 years you have a hell of a record, but there's got to be a point at which you level. Most people go through that – Colin has been lucky not to go through it before – and then come back. It's just one of those things.

Colin is under pressure to win a major. Does he have to work extra hard to control the negative effect that could have?

I would like to think that he doesn't. I'd like to think he treats a major like any other tournament, but inevitably there is more pressure there. You just have to make sure you are finely tuned leading into those majors.

It's not only about playing well beforehand, it's doing every-thing you can so you go in hitting the same ball as in any other competition. If you allow it to be something different, you're allowing media and public pressure to control your game.

Colin says he is trying to 'unlearn' his temperament. Does that mean he thinks his temperament has had a negative impact on his performance?

I think there may be a little bit of that. But sometimes it's to do with how you expect your image to be as a professional golfer and as an entertainer. I think we have to be very careful not to confuse those two things. The guy has been top for seven consecutive years – so how much has his temperament affected his game? I would say zero.

I do find it interesting, though, that the media very rarely focus on the things that I see Tiger Woods doing – and he does some pretty outrageous things when he is playing badly. You see him throwing clubs and things like that, but they leave him alone. So why do they pick on Colin? And they do, because I've looked at this carefully.

I've said to myself: how many bad things has Tiger Woods done today? Perhaps three or four. Colin? One. Anything about Tiger? Nil. Everything is about Colin. Now why is that?

How important might it be that Colin is now happier playing in the States?

I think it's critical. I was there with him in Cleveland in August and there was a huge difference in the crowds. That was to do with his weight and everything else. Fundamentally that means you are playing on your home territory.

What part do you feel you've played in his success?

I'm part of the team. But what I've brought to his game is a very good, firm foundation. And I've also established what I call winning strategies, and those have come from my knowledge of being a coach at the highest levels.

That is the most critical thing. We've all got our bits to play as team members, but I just think I've done my bit very effectively. I also bring something from outside – I don't play golf.

---

ball that can take you from third to winning. I didn't putt as well as I have – whether that's fortune or ability I'm not sure. But I haven't lost my game."

This, though, is now very much a topic of hot debate. Some observers are already writing Monty off as the pre-eminent force in European golf, and heralding Lee Westwood as its new crown prince.

Others are not so sure. Team Monty – his coach Paul Marchand and his psychologist

Hugh Mantle – will tell you that last year amounted to an "inconsistency of results" rather than a slump in their man's confidence or game. Which is what you'd expect them to say.

What is interesting about talking to Monty now, though, is this sense that losing his number one status has come partly as a relief to him. But only because it frees him up to focus on that other "great strain" – his failure to win a major.

I ask him if his plan to spend extra time in the States this year – a week of preparation before both the US Open and USPGA Championship – is a serious statement of intent that he's targeting the majors in 2001.

"Of course it is," he says after a lengthy pause. "Hopefully I've nothing to prove in Europe now. Right? If I can win other Dutch Opens, French Opens or German Opens, yes, okay, I won the tournament. But at the same time it's not going to change..." he halts midflow.

"A major wouldn't change my life. It would change a statement about me. Rather than 'Monty was good *but...*' it would change to 'Monty was good *and...*' And that would be the statement I'd like to finish my career on.

"I just feel I owe it to myself now," he says of his plans for the States. "Just to see if it might swing it a wee bit. That one shot here and there, that's all it is."

His analysis is accurate. One shot here or there is all it takes at the top level. But his tone is tentative, and you can't help thinking that this whole 'greatest player never to win a major' tag might have led Monty, in his quiet moments, to feel an uncomfortable anticipation that indeed he never will.

Who can blame him? Having come close at the 1992 US Open (Jack Nicklaus had already congratulated him on victory before Tom Kite snatched it from his grasp), feeling the pain of play-off defeat in the 1994 US Open and 1995 USPGA Championship, and then finishing runner-up to Ernie Els in the 1997 US Open, Monty must wonder what he has to do. The answer now, worryingly for him, is to beat the best golfers in the world – and then beat Tiger Woods.

But will an extra week here and there really make a big impact on his chances? Talk to 1970 US Open champion Tony Jacklin and he'll tell you that you need to play the whole season Stateside. Monty has been roundly criticised, of course, for not having played more in the US. Not only to prepare for the majors, but to prove himself a world class golfer. Nick Faldo, never short of advice, opined publicly that the Scot should go west. But Monty has always maintained that he would rather stay home with his family.

Mind you, America has never been a happy hunting ground for him. He knew that when he crossed the pond, the galleries would be waiting for him. Monty baiting – calling him names because of his weight – became a popular sport among more raucous spectators, who revelled in seeing how much it irritated him. It all culminated at the 1999 Ryder Cup.

"It was horrific, horrendous," reflects Monty

> "Losing weight has affected my self-esteem. When my wife and I go out, I feel better about myself. People say you are looking good, and your chest sticks out a bit."

"Horrific, horrendous." That's how Monty looks back on his treatment at Ryder Cup 1999.

frankly. "I wouldn't wish that on anybody. It was the hardest time of my career. But I came out of it. And the press afterwards was quite unbelievable, in my favour. The American public decided then, I think: 'Hang on, we've given this guy an extra hard time and he's come out and beaten us at our own game; and right, we'll

Monty sits dejected, realising the pack has caught up with him at the Volvo Masters.

respect him.'

"And the last time I was over there, with the weight loss as well, it was good. I found it at Pebble Beach and at the Masters – people were respecting me."

His weight. It seems odd that Monty should have won over America not only through his golfing genius, but through dietary self-discipline too. It becomes apparent, however, that shedding two and a half stones by cutting out his favourite fatty foods has been immensely important to the way he sees himself.

"It's the self-esteem," he reveals. "I've won tournaments three or four stones heavier than I am now – and I played well at the World Matchplay at this weight. So it doesn't affect my golf at all. What it does affect is your self-esteem, and it raises confidence levels – especially when you do your job in public as I do.

"When my wife and I go out, around town or whatever, I feel better about myself now. People say you are looking good, and your chest sticks out a bit."

It's bizarre to think of a millionaire golfer, the best in Europe, suffering from a low sense of self-worth. But that is precisely what Monty is hinting at. I ask if all the name-calling ever hurt him.

"Some people's comments have hurt. I get..." I'm anticipating the word 'down', but he checks himself and tries to put a positive spin on the subject... "Being in the public eye you get immune to it. You can't live by someone's opinion of you."

But Monty also talks about no longer having to "hide within himself", which is hardly the sentiment of a man immune to personal criticism. I sense that the harsh words have hit home, and Colin Montgomerie is a more sensitive individual than he'd like us to believe.

However, while you could never find a man guilty for being the butt of such personal jokes, it's hard to construct a defence for Monty when it comes to his temperament. It's at the very heart of why he seems to attract such ambivalent reactions from the golfing public, even here in Britain. He is exasperating to watch. In any given round he can have the galleries cheering him on as approach after approach lands inches from the stick; then scattering as Monty sees red and starts firing like a loose cannon.

I've been wondering how to broach this sensitive subject, but he proves pretty straight about it. I ask him if there have been times when his temperament has had a negative impact on his play.

"I think so, yes, and you regret these situations. But at the same time, over the last two or three years that situation has lessened considerably."

Worried that this improvement may have gone unnoticed by the rest of the world, I ask him to define his temperament now. The answer is intriguing.

"How would I define my temperament?" he ponders. "You can unlearn a temperament. If it's learnt, you can unlearn it. And I think I'm learning to unlearn it, in a way."

That sounds like psychobabble, but I take it to mean that he has tried, and continues trying, to control his temper on-course. Further probing, however, is deflected with cheery answers that have nothing whatever to do with the question.

So is Monty guilty of letting himself down by losing his rag on the golf course? Despite protestations that he's a changed man, you'd have to say the evidence – and last November's Volvo Masters is a case in point – is stacked against him.

But his psychologist, Dr Hugh Mantle, makes an interesting point in mitigation. He says: "Most people will say what a temper John McEnroe had. But did it affect his game? I think the answer is no – no, completely.

"Players who are great perfectionists and want to achieve so much do get very upset about things quickly. What I find, though, is that they are then able to switch off from that. But I think they still feel they are letting themselves down because of how their image comes across."

The problem perhaps lies in the fact that for Monty, golf is a job, whereas for spectators it is sport and entertainment. The conventions which govern those activities do not necessarily match. So while Monty's performance may not be hugely affected by a bad mood, we are British, cough-cough, and there are certain unwritten rules to be adhered to. We'd rather not see that sort of thing on the golf course, thank you very much.

Dr Mantle, it emerges, has been a pivotal figure in Monty's career throughout his years of success. He is a leading psychologist at Liverpool's John Moores University and a successful Olympic coach, and Monty speaks to him by phone every day during a tournament.

"He's been working with me for seven years now, but I keep it quite quiet, I don't make a big issue of it," Monty reveals. "It's the first time I've mentioned it much, really. But without him I wouldn't have won what I've won."

How has Monty benefited, I wonder?

"Preparation. He gets you prepared for the first tee of a tournament. If you are not prepared to succeed, you have prepared to fail. Right? And that's why we have been so successful – because we have prepared to succeed."

And what does he do, precisely, to prepare to succeed?

"Er... I would rather not say," replies Monty, eyeing me keenly. "That's between him and me, to be honest. But there's been a lot that's had to be learned."

It's interesting that such profound psychology is seen by Monty as a cornerstone of his success. Can it really make a meaningful difference?

"Of course it can," he says assertively. "Especially at my level. One shot and I would have won three majors by now. I'd have won four times last year instead of twice. It goes on and on and on."

Thinking about those majors again? You bet he is.

Colin Montgomerie is a golfer who, despite his unprecedented success in Europe over the past decade, has come in for lots of criticism and faces a longer list of 'charges' than most. Lee Westwood isn't averse to doing a Mr Grouchy on his day, yet we still wish him well. Darren Clarke beat Tiger Woods in a World Golf Championship final, yet he's not asked every week when he will be smoking his first major cigar. And we've even learned to love funny old Mr Faldo a little by now, comedy trip-ups and all. So why is it so hard to love Monty?

Perhaps it's because all these players are somehow seen as entertainers and heroes in the surreal world that is professional sport. Monty, on the other hand, is just doing his job – albeit in a highly efficient and competitive way. "If I was working in a bank," he has said in the past, "I'd be competitive." And he would.

It seems that the 'just doing my job' philosophy doesn't quite hack it for golf fans. We don't expect our sports stars to go home at 5.30pm. So I wonder if the most serious charge against Colin Montgomerie is that he doesn't love golf. It's a question I put to him.

Four slow-motion seconds pass before he answers.

"I love the competition, and I'm lucky to be able to do something that's competitive. I would be competitive in any business – it just happens to be golf that I have a great ability for, and that has given me a great, great life. You ask me do I love golf... yes, of course I do."

Somehow I'm not entirely convinced by this answer. Maybe Monty feels he's forced to say it, because if he tried to explain his deeper sentiments, it would be misconstrued by the golfing public and sensationalised by the press. Whatever, we have to take his word for it.

It's symptomatic, though, of a strange sensation I'm getting from this meeting. Monty has been relaxed, smiley and polite. My questions have been carefully considered and answered articulately. However, there's a sense of remoteness about him that I can't quite put my finger on. It's a bit like I've been talking to a television

presenter, meticulously mindful of his style, delivery and image.

It could just be his way of dealing with journalists, scripting the answers a bit and not letting anyone get too close. But I'm aware that in the short time we've been talking, I'm not entirely sure which bits are the real Monty and which are not.

I round off the interview by asking him if he has long-term plans.

"Not really. I'm still playing tournament golf, I'm still top ten in the world, so nothing long-term apart from looking forward to my family growing up. Right? Being healthy and having a fulfilled life and doing the golf course development stuff, which I enjoy. And winning the odd tournament – that's okay with me.

"Nothing will change my lifestyle now – winning a golf tournament, a major or otherwise – it's not going to change me in any shape or form. Yes, it would be nice to say 'Monty was good and...' rather than 'Monty was good but he never won a major,' but it won't change me one way or another if I happen to win a major or not. Not at all."

Right?

The stress shows, as a chubby-looking Monty goes down in a play-off at the 1994 US Open.

The new slimline version in happier mood after an eagle at Valderrama last November.

THE COACH
Paul Marchand

You've worked with Colin for two years now – what is he like as a person?

Something that is not appreciated much is his terrific sense of humour – he really likes to carry on and have a good laugh now and then. He's been portrayed as this serious-minded guy, but he's really not like that most of the time.

He's very interested in a lot of things. He knows an awful lot about automobiles and is a big music fan. He has an interest in politics and is well spoken on many different subjects.

Did you spot anything in Colin's game last year that might have led to his dip in results?

I didn't see an area of his game that looked different, other than the natural ups and downs of golf itself. When I saw him play he played very well. It wasn't as if he was off his game. Everyone likes to bring out the slump word. It just wasn't happening.

How hard does he practise?

Well, what I like is that when he practises, he practises really hard. He's not the kind of guy to hit balls for three hours for the sake of it. He's goes out there with a purpose and to work with intensity. But when Colin's playing well, he's more likely to put the clubs away and get ready for the next day. He's smart like that.

Colin has a natural swing – like your other pupil, Fred Couples.

Absolutely. Fred and Colin have a lot in common. Colin's a feel player and he trusts his mechanics – the way he's swung the club all his life. I feel a little bit of self-knowledge goes a long way.

He doesn't have to understand everything, nor does he want to. It's my job to help with that self-knowledge, to show him the cause and effect of a shot without getting into the mechanics.

Colin has come under fire for his temperament over the years. Is that something you have talked to him about?

My interpretation, from listening to him, is that he feels he has been very honest. He really does say what he thinks, and he reacts to shots and situations the way he is truly feeling.

When you are a very public person and you are being judged constantly by people, the consequences of being open and honest sometimes come back and bite you, and it hurts.

Monty's coach describes him as a 'feel' player.

MARK JAMES

GOLF WORLD — As originally published October 2002

Rebel with a Cause

Blazing rows, apathy and wild celebration. **Mark James** has had a 23-year love-hate relationship with the Ryder Cup. He's still up for a fight in 2002.

MARK JAMES HAS ALWAYS BEEN A STUBBORN BUGGER. To say he relishes an argument would be like suggesting Genghis Khan was quite keen on a weekend away with the lads or that Oliver Reed was partial to the occasional half-pint of shandy. This is not a slight on James's character. In fact, it is to be applauded, plays a major part in his make-up, and James, with a twinkle in his eye and a rye smile, really rather enjoys his mischievous streak.

First impressions with James deceive and his appearance doesn't help his cause – as if he could care. His deadpan, slow, cowboy drawl and the trademark droopy moustache, which pulls his smile-shy mouth still further down his face, makes him look and sound down in the mouth. With his shiny, egg-shaped pate, he appears, worryingly, to be morphing into Jean-Luc Picard, captain of the modern

Star Trek USS Enterprise. Even more worrying is that James is a proud and fully-paid up member of the Star Trek fan club and has a certificate to prove it hanging on the wall in his snooker room. He even bunked off to watch his favourite programme once when he should have been defending himself at a disciplinary hearing. "I honestly can't believe I did that," he grins. "I certainly didn't do myself any favours."

James has one of those slow-burning mickey-taking sense of humours that is often misread, and because, as he admits, he isn't a smiley person, he often appears moody and unapproachable. You feel he is really rather happy not to dispel any of these observations, either. "I'm just not a smiler," he half-smiles, cheekily. Yet James is one of the friendliest and most accommodating players on tour. This tired, hang-dog image is a smokescreen.

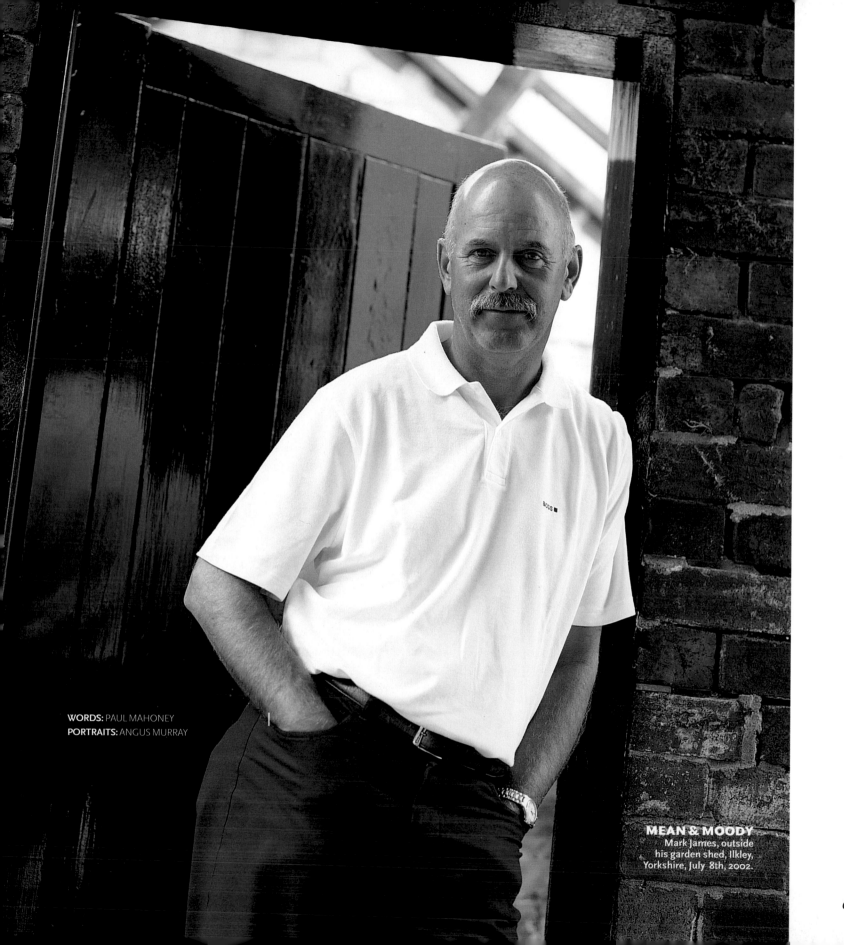

WORDS: PAUL MAHONEY
PORTRAITS: ANGUS MURRAY

MEAN & MOODY
Mark James, outside
his garden shed, Ilkley,
Yorkshire, July 8th, 2002.

SOME MIGHT THINK MARK JAMES courted controversy for the first time by writing his book, Into The Bear Pit, about his experiences as Ryder Cup captain at Brookline in 1999. The row that ensued when he revealed how he had thrown away a good luck message from Nick Faldo meant he was forced to resign as Sam Torrance's vice-captain for this year's matches at the Belfry. He will still be an assistant though, adding he never really put any importance on titles. Which suggests his role will remain the same. But Faldo kept going on about it in the Press, James says "and had to be told by the committee to shut up – which was brilliant. Nick and I are obviously oil and water and we are probably going to have to agree to disagree. As far as I'm concerned, all that is finished."

James answered his calling to wage a one-man crusade against 'the system' from an early age. Born in 1953 in Manchester he was brought up in Stamford, Lincolnshire, discovering golf when he was 12. "I always had a sense of timing," he says. "But it was not always obvious with my short, lashing swing." This honest analysis of his own game is also a fitting description of the way his bluntness has often got him into sticky situations. He admits to being pathetic at school, shy and a bad communicator. He kept getting chucked out of class so he spent most of his time staring at the wall out in the corridor or writing out pages of lines. "I was a bit of a loony," he says, grinning in an oh-well-what-the-heck kind of way. But if you think this makes him a drop-out fool, you'd be wrong. He passed nine O Levels and then his father (who worked his way through the ranks to become managing director of Pedigree Pet Foods) struck a deal that if he studied hard for his A Levels, he would fund him for a season on the full amateur tour. James passed mathematics and economics, won the English Amateur Championship in 1974 and was picked for the Walker Cup team the following year. He turned pro in 1976 giving himself five years to make it or he would walk away. "I just couldn't bear to work in an office," he says. He needn't have worried. He finished 15th on tour and was Rookie of the Year. He made his Ryder Cup debut the following season at Royal Lytham and has now won 18 European Tour events and amassed £3.5 million in prize money. He has rarely played on the US Tour "because of all the travel and the lack of fish and chip shops".

The house he and wife Jane own in a tucked away corner of Ilkley in Yorkshire is a successful-looking yet normal pile with none of the pretentious trappings often associated with the mock-Tudor trophy homes loved by footballers with too much money and not enough style. "I realise how lucky I am not to have a proper job," he says. "When I joined the tour there wasn't that

much money in golf. I did reasonably well for about 12 years and had a house, a mortgage and cars but I had accumulated no money at all. Yet his financial future was assured when prize money escalated in the Eighties and the Ryder Cup became enormous. Their kitchen has recently been extended and is a spotless ("Jane can't stand clutter") yet far from crassly luxurious show-house affair. The relative normality of the James household and lifestyle is further proved when he admits the curtains in the TV lounge are about 10 years old. "Have you seen the bloody price of curtains?"

This no-nonsense, down-to-earth, northern brashness was irritating the creases in the blazers of the largely southern-run

tour from early in James's career. It wasn't long before he was hauled before the tournament committee and fined for pulling out of an event. "It was ridiculous. I had no caddie and a bad knee." His card was marked as his anti-establishment attitudes and lack of respect for what he perceived as undeserved authority gained infamy in the corridors of power. But it was at the Ryder Cup at the Greenbrier, Virginia in 1979 that tempers were lost, egos clashed and a commitment by James was made to fight a system he believed often failed to relate to or support him and the younger players.

"When Ken Brown and I started playing in the Ryder Cup, the team got slaughtered (that's beaten heavily not heavily drunk, obviously) pretty much every match. And there were people involved who didn't have too much time for youngsters like me and Ken. There was a bit of a witch hunt in 1979. It was very wrong. A list of misdemeanours attributed to me was produced. It was just

"There was a witch hunt at the Ryder Cup in 1979. There was a long list of misdemeanours attributed to me. You couldn't make it up. It was so wrong"

DOUBLE ACT
Mark James and Ken Brown, Ryder Cup debuts, Royal Lytham, 1977.
"You'd have got good odds on us being captain and assistant in 1999."

Mark James on...

TEAM MEETINGS
They'll be at about 6 o'clock every evening. Sam will announce the pairings, discuss tactics and find out how everyone is feeling. We haven't quite got to using blackboards like in football changing rooms yet – but maybe in another 10 years!

THIS YEAR'S ATMOSPHERE
I can't see it being soft and lovely. There were sporting events taking place in America six days after September 11. Professional sports people are not capable of going out to compete and not giving 110%. This is how we are made. But just because there will be an edge, it doesn't mean everyone has forgotten about September 11. Nor should we.

CROWD BEHAVIOUR
Just like after Kiawah in 1991 and Brookline in 1999, it is falling on us to make sure our crowd behaves well to make up for the American excesses. There will never be any big problems over here. I'm not saying there are not a few cheers and comments when there shouldn't be. That is bound to happen. But it is blatantly obvious, even to the dimmest of minds, when things go over the top.

ludicrous. I was supposed to have got on the aeroplane in jeans and trainers which is not true. I had the team suit on but I was just wearing a pair of suede shoes instead of the official leather ones. But I had packed them in my carry bag in case they were needed for a photograph. I just didn't want my feet to hurt walking through airports in new shoes. Then I was accused of flicking food during a team dinner. That wasn't me; that was another member of the team. Again, it was crazy saying I was late for the

> **"** I don't like being trodden on. And I don't like others being trodden on. And I don't like people who try to rail-rode other people **"**

opening ceremony – that was rubbish. There were accusations of not turning up for a team meeting, too, but Ken and I were only told about it when we were out practising so by the time we got back to the clubhouse, we were a little late. There is just a long list of stuff. You couldn't make it up. It was done by people because, well, they didn't like me." He pauses. "Which is fine."

But it clearly is not fine – and James's tone became increasingly annoyed, recounting the way in which he felt he had been hard done by. He admits he calls a spade a spade and, even from his amateur days, he has never really identified with the cocktail party, blazer brigade side of golf. "I just

don't like authority that says one thing for no good reason. There is nothing worse than that 'Because I say so' mentality. That really annoys me – just a bit," he says slowly. For "just a bit" read "quite a lot". James was working himself up into a frenzy. Each word was punctuated by a pause for dramatic effect, emphasising the anger that still eats away inside him at the way he has been treated. "It. Makes. My. Blood. Boil," he says, managing to stop himself from banging on the table with his fist. James has tensed up and he is one angry man. He laughs to diffuse the tension.

James has never been shy of expressing his opinion, even if it proves unpopular. In his follow-up book about the Ryder Cup and all that has happened to him since (After the Bear Pit), he admits he sometimes goes too far defending things he feels passionate about. "I will defend my point of view – or someone else's – vigorously if I think it is right. I don't like being trodden on. And I don't like other people being trodden on. And I don't like people who try to rail-rode other people because of who they are or because they think they have a God-given right to have their own way."

He's back tub-thumping again like the avenging good-guy gunslinger standing on the bar in the saloon and swearing he's gonna clean up this dirty, stinkin' neighbourhood and run the bad guys outta town – a rebel with a cause.

So just how the hell did James get to wear the sheriff's badge? How the hell did Jesse James get to be the law man? Quite incredibly, considering his track record, James was voted in as chairman of the players' committee in 1995 and, completing his poacher turned gamekeeper turnaround, he was chosen as Ryder Cup captain for the 1999 matches at Brookline and chose Ken Brown as his assistant. "You'd have got good odds on that ever happening," James laughs. "It might have been Tony Jacklin who said I wasn't suitable for the job because of what happened at Greenbrier in 1979. I mean, Christ Almighty, that was 20 years ago. You can kill someone and not get 20 years. It's laughable. Incredible."

James has become an authority figure on tour but that does not mean he has diluted his strong beliefs. He insists he is still his own man. "I haven't changed.

"Players are treated more fairly these days. But if you've been throwing clubs then it's a fair cop"

I won't shy away from standing my corner in an argument. You need a bit of gumption if you don't want to be walked over." He believes the players have an advantage by having him represent them. He says that, rather than exercising authority over them, he is giving it back to them. "Putting some of it back onto the wrong side of the fence. That's where I would have liked to have seen it when I started playing." He hasn't forgotten how ostracised he felt when he turned pro and even now he sees the players' side as the "wrong side".

James is still fighting the good fight and his rebellious streak is as strong as ever. All of which, with a track record such as his, must cause problems when he has to chastise the new breed of brash young rebels. Like Sergio Garcia, for example. "If they've been screaming obscenities or throwing clubs, then it's a fair cop, and they just have to cough up their fine." But he insists players are treated a lot more fairly these days because the tour staff are more lenient and attempt to understand them. Plus his tournament committee is very representative of the players and may well come down on their side in an appeal.

HAVING RESOLVED his differences with Faldo and Jacklin, saying he doesn't bare grudges, "The Witch Hunt At Greenbrier" still sticks in his throat and writing his book doesn't seem to have exorcised its ghosts, either. "I wanted to tell how wrong it all was; tell my side of the story. It was nice to get it all down on paper but that doesn't mean I'm not still annoyed." James pauses to gather himself. He is getting angry. His blood is starting to boil again. His words are delivered like single gunshots, slamming across the kitchen table. "Because. I. Hate. People. Lying." He sounded frustrated and exasperated. "I can't believe it. They were such ridiculous lies." He pulls himself back from the brink. "Actually, I'm still annoyed. You can tell, can't you?" He laughs at the situation and himself. His self-deprecating humour again is his comfort blanket.

That humour was severely tested again in August 2000 when James had a rather more serious battle against the system. He was diagnosed with cancer. But his first reaction to this news, he reveals in After

the Bear Pit, was: "Damn, no skiing for me this year." That was typical of the man. After a year of treatment (Faldo even sent a get well card), allied to his appetite for a fight, James made a full recovery. When many people pull through life-threatening ordeals, they often come out the other side softer, calmer and simply happy to be alive. Not surprisingly, James swims against the tide. "It hasn't changed me at all. I seem to be exactly the same – unfortunately," he laughs. "I did wonder what I would be like. I was aware that psychologically it might be difficult getting back on tour and I might feel differently. Being so aware of that, there was less chance of it happening."

James hits 50 in October 2003 and is looking forward to another lease of life on the European Seniors Tour. You'd think a man of his age would be slowing down, chilling out. Of course, he isn't. But what on earth has he got left to fight for? Just what is his cause these days? James pauses and you can feel the mischief brewing inside his head. A slow, lip-curling Elvis Presley smile grows from the corner of his mouth. "Truth, justice and the European way," he announces in his best John Wayne drawl. He laughs at the absurdity of it all. "I just like picking fights," he adds. I do like arguing. I wouldn't do things just for a fight but I really do hate injustice."

James has picked many scraps throughout his career but, he admits, his biggest error of judgement had nothing to do with golf. "I was foolish. I took a bit of a risk," he explains, suppressing a smirk. "My main career mistake was not planting my runner beans early enough and the frost got them. It's a mistake I've never repeated."

HOME FRONT
Not a mock-Tudor pillar in sight: "I can relax here in about 10 minutes."

Mark James on...

BACKROOM STAFF
Woosie, me and Joakim Haeggman will be Sam's eyes and ears. We'll be buzzing around, spending time with each group, getting to know how they are playing, thinking, and coping with the course.

BELFRY PAIRINGS
Most are fairly obvious: Harrington and McGinley, Westwood and Clarke. But if one of them is playing badly that might change. We have a young team who will be able to play a lot and won't mind who they partner. In the past, certain players have said they don't want to play on Saturday afternoon. That won't happen.

CAPTAIN SAM
The buck stops with Sam. I don't think it is any easier for him to be captain this time than it is difficult for me to be an assistant. Sam is a friend whose judgement I trust implicitly.

BROOKLINE LESSONS
Being more aware of how much the players can play and how they may get tired – not physically but mentally. It's too easy to say some should have been rested while others should have played. It is easily countered that it was worth it to go into the singles with a four-point lead.

Justin Rose

Blooming lovely

From that pitch-in as an amateur at the 1998 Open, to 21 missed cuts in a row, to England's No.1. It's been an incredible journey for Justin Rose. And he's still only 21.

WORDS: PAUL MAHONEY   **MAIN PHOTOGRAPHY:** JAMES CHEADLE

I T IS TWO-AND-A-HALF HOURS SINCE England's footballers ambled to their bore draw with Nigeria to qualify for the second round of the World Cup finals, and England's No.1 golfer is nowhere to be seen.

He cruises into the car park at Stoke Park Golf Club, Berkshire, in his sponsored Jaguar 20 minutes late. "I asked for a black Jag because it looks cool," Rose says later. "It's got red leather seats so it's a little bit funky and it stands out from the crowd but, at the same time, it's not too flashy." It is said that you can tell much about someone's character by the car they drive. For this 21-year old, who admits "it is nice to be young – and feel old", he seems to have made the perfect choice.

Rose has just moved into his first house – a modest six-bedrooms in Fleet, Hampshire – and blames his tardiness

PHIL SHELDON

on the fact that he couldn't find his shoes. "Everything is packed in boxes," he apologises, grinning. "I don't know where anything is. But then he came clean. "And, er, I've been watching the football on TV with my mum and dad. Sorry!" Fair enough, then. Who can blame him?

When Nick Faldo won the Open in 1987 he did so with 18 straight pars at Muirfield. His critics (and there were plenty) said it was dull but the record books will show Faldo was the champion golfer that July. Tiger Woods, too, won the Masters and the US Open this year not by blasting away on the final day but by playing the percentages, laying up and realising par was all he had to get. "England's performance against Nigeria was very Faldoesque," Rose says. "They knew that par was good enough to get through and that's what they got. Nothing flashy, but they got the job done." Having learned from his

Justin Rose, recreating that 1998 Birkdale moment, Stoke Park Golf Club, Berkshire, June 5th, 2002: "I guess that's what everyone remembers me for."

FIRST BIG HIT
Rose (far right) wins
the British Masters at
Woburn, May 2002,
pipping his mate Ian
Poulter. It was the end
of a four-year quest to
become England's
No.1 golfer.

FIRST BIG MISS
Justin-mania at the
Dutch Open, July 1998:
the start of his dreadful
run of 21 missed cuts.

topsy-turvy experiences on the world's golf courses, Rose sympathises with the dilemma that faced England's footballers. "After such a great performance like the one against Argentina, it is often difficult to raise your game again so soon," he says. "Despite all the team talks by Sven-Goran Eriksson telling them to go for a win, in the back of their heads they still knew a draw would be good enough – so then critics say their performance wasn't so good."

Rose's form this season has been very typically English. "It has been crazy: missed cut, then really good performance, then missed cut, then really good performance. But I'd rather miss nine cuts and win nine times than finish 20th 18 times. It's more fun that way. I don't panic now if I have a bad week. I have belief in my game, which is down to all the hard work I've put in over the last couple of years."

Rose is riding along on this unexpected wave of British success in Golden Jubilee year: David Beckham wreaking revenge on Argentina, Lennox Lewis battering Mike Tyson, our cricketers finally scoring runs and the annual high-pitched jamboree of Henman-mania at Wimbledon. Rose has made a significant breakthrough this season, winning three times around the world and then bagging his first victory on home soil at the British Masters at Woburn in June. He has ousted Lee Westwood and Nick Faldo as England's No.1 golfer, is 7th on the European Order of Merit and 44th in the world. "I feel I have moved up to the next level," he says. "I'm in the elite top 50, mentally stronger and making fewer errors. I am looking forward to competing in majors. You know, I nearly won one once!"

That image of Rose after he had pitched in at the last hole to finish fourth at the Open at Royal Birkdale in 1998 will stay with him for the rest of his life. It was his last shot as an amateur and it is still the one thing everyone asks him about. "That picture is great," he beams. "It was a fantastic week that I will always remember." But it must irritate him that every time he puts himself back into the limelight, that moment comes out of the archives. He must be sick of the sight of it. "I am a little bit," he smiles, "but it was a piece of history. You can't knock it! I always thought the thing that would stop people talking about it would be my first win. But it hasn't. I suppose that's what they remember me for."

Having established that Rose seems happy to still talk about that defining moment in his life, the time seemed right to ask if he would like to recreate it. "That would be great," he smiles. "I've never been asked to do that before. It will be a unique picture." So, standing on a wall in the back garden of Stoke Park Golf Club, Rose clutched a sand wedge in his left hand and laughed his head off, just like he did after that that final pitch at Birkdale darted into the hole. There was such hysteria surrounding Rose that tour veteran Wayne Riley dubbed him Baby Spice. "For quite a time after the Open, a lot of people were interested in me, probably because it was such a bizarre thing that happened," Rose says, trying to keep his balance. "I'm signing more autographs at golf courses now but I don't get recognised so regularly on the streets. Some people come up to me and say: 'You're that golfer, aren't you?' My face still rings a bell but they don't know my name."

But that skinny, grinning little 17-year-old, high-fiving the galleries, has travelled a long and winding road in the past four years. He is one of Britain's top sporting prospects now but he can still go down the pub in his jeans and a t-shirt and be one of the boys. When Rose left school, every single person signed his year book and wrote: 'Good luck, see you when

> I can still go down to the pub in my jeans and t-shirt with my mates. But the first round is always on me – and they make sure it's a big one. I don't mind though!

"I feel I've moved up to the next level. I'm mentally stronger."

Justin's 'Terminator' look: despite all the setbacks he knew he'd be back.

Rose's motto "don't get mad, get even" saw him through the dark days.

> "Looking back at all those missed cuts, obviously I wasn't very happy. I was spending hours on the range and getting nowhere"

you are rich and famous!' They are all still genuine mates and Rose says they are a reality check for him, too. "The first round is always on me," he laughs, "and they make sure it's a big one. But I really don't mind. Some of them are still studying; others are bricklayers and carpenters. I'm the one with the weird job and luckily I get paid a lot of money. But I did make sacrifices – I didn't go down the pub as much as they did!"

His mates would surely give him stick if they knew he was sporting a Versace belt for his *Golf World* photoshoot. "Well, there's a funny story behind the belt," he offers in his defence. "I was in Japan and got up one day and my old belt somehow wouldn't fit anymore. So I went to a shop and just picked one up and put it on the counter. It was 50,000 yen, or something like that, which meant absolutely nothing to me. I didn't notice it was a designer label. But then when I got home I worked out it cost me £260. What a rip off!" Rose may be a millionaire now but he is still down to earth enough to know when he has been fleeced. "It is nice that when I go shopping, I can buy whatever I like without having to think too hard," he says. "But it is important to have a sense of value. I have been brought up that way and I am sure my family and friends will keep me that way."

LIFE IS SWEET FOR ROSE RIGHT NOW. HIS dreams are coming true and he is beginning to realise his potential. "I was sitting at home the

other night with my mum and dad and was thinking: 'Well, you know, on paper, there is no better player than me in England. You think of all the amateurs and professionals and the millions of people who play golf, and I'm No.1." Rose says this not in a boastful way, but in a delighted, joyful and modest way. He has certainly kept his feet on the ground and can thank his mates and parents and their close-knit family for making him such a mature, well-rounded 21-year-old. "I am probably a bit more serious than that 17-year-old you all saw at Birkdale. But I still like to go around a golf course and give something back to the fans. In pro golf you have to be more focussed to perform every week. But that's not to say you can't smile!" Rose smiles.

But life on tour wasn't always a laughing matter for Rose. A week after the Open at Birkdale, he teed it up in the Dutch Open as a professional for the first time. He won the pro-am and a cheque for £625. It would be his last winner's pay day for a very long time. He missed the cut by one shot – a spectacular second round 65 failing to rescue a nervy first round 77. Each week, the media circus and his new-found fans turned up to pop open the champagne, and each week the pressure weighed ever more heavily on his young shoulders as he failed to deliver and his tournament invites began to dry up. Two missed cuts ran into eight, then 13, then 17, then 21. Some players, also struggling to make a living and jealous of the attention and help Rose was receiving, began to call him Just Invite. Rose was dabbling with several sets of irons after signing a £600,000 contract with Taylor Made and he grew taller by almost three inches by the end of August. His swing, basically, needed to be re-invented to fit around his new body and it took his father, and coach David Leadbetter a long time to put things right.

"I don't really know what was going on in my head," Justin says. "I blanked a lot of it out. I try to take the positives out of it but, looking back, obviously I wasn't happy. I was spending hours on the range and getting nowhere." There was no relief or sense of achievement even when Rose finally made the weekend for the first time at the European Grand Prix at Slaley Hall, 11 months later in June 1999. Rose was in the first group out and needed a par at the last to make the cut but missed the green with his approach.

"It was probably one of the best up-and-downs I have ever made," he says. "I hit a great pitch to six feet and had to hole a putt with about one foot of swing. I really sensed the pressure. I remember one of my playing partners, Fredrik Jacobsen, being so pleased for me when the ball fell into the hole. I played terribly and finished last. I thought, 'Well, making the cut is not all it's cracked up to be!'" he laughed. But he survived those dark days armed with the determination and patience he says he has inherited from his father, a personal motto that says: 'Don't get mad, get even', a sense of humour, a hard work ethic, steely belief in his considerable talent and an admitted maturity beyond his years.

It has been a remarkable turnaround for Rose, one that many others would have lacked the guts to pull through despite all the setbacks. But it is a journey Rose has taken admirably in his stride and he looks to be enjoying himself and is confident in the limelight. "I remember how bad it used to be. You might as well enjoy it when you are up there," he says. "You always feel pressure and nerves but I really enjoy the challenge of dealing with it. I am very calm about it all. Having not won before and then winning four times in five months is amazing. It is sort of 'pinch yourself stuff' but I feel quite comfortable with it. But I still need to keep working hard on my game and re-evaluating my goals."
THOSE GOALS INCLUDE COMPETING IN the majors and challenging Tiger Woods. "To play against him would do my maturing process good because you are going to learn a lot about yourself and how you deal with all that goes on around him," Rose says. "I would like to think I could give him a run for his money." Rose got as near to Woods as he has since Royal Birkdale in 1998 (Rose was fourth to Woods' third) when he finished one shot off joining the play-off at the Deutsche Bank International in May in which Woods defeated Colin Montgomerie. "I certainly competed well with two of the best players in the world," Rose says. "I was pretty satisfied with the way I played."

To compete on that level regularly, Rose recognises there are further changes that need to take place. One of which is to get fitter in the gym and to be more careful about his diet – which, presumably, he hasn't

"I feel comfortable on tour now. I know the ropes."

started yet, unless the bacon sarnie he ordered was of the fat-free variety. But, most importantly, he realises his game is not yet good enough – an honest, modest and yet ambitious revelation. "I need to learn to play more variety of shots: different distance shots with my wedges, greenside chips with a 3-wood, that little knock-down 2-iron that Tiger hits. Little things like that will give me back one or two more strokes which will get me to the next level," he says.

When he arrived on tour, Rose admits he felt like he stuck out a bit. The spotlight under which he had to perform was so intense it is not surprising that, at times, he looked like a rabbit caught in the headlights of an oncoming Volvo. But he says he is managing his time better now, knows the ropes, how to practise, when to arrive at a tournament and he has learned how to play the courses.

Rose certainly knows where he wants to be and what it will take to get there. Judging by the way he has plugged away and fought hard to become England's No.1, only a fool would bet against him reaching the very top of his profession. He has a real chance of becoming the first English golfer to win a major six years after Nick Faldo became the last, winning the Masters at Augusta in 1996.

When Rose was about 10 years old, he says he was often sent home from school for being naughty. But then he discovered golf and, unlike many frustrated weekend golfers, he finds playing it chills him out. He has certainly had his patience tested on the golf course over the years and admits to channelling his still youthful energy into driving his Jaguar. "I can get a bit impatient and aggressive," he says, smiling. "But I can stay calm on the golf course."

Despite his sense of fun, you can feel that Rose possesses that killer instinct crucial for any successful athlete. "I love to look somebody in the eye and know that's the guy I've got to beat," he says. Goofing for the camera, he pretends to get all serious so he can give us his 'let's get ready to rumble' Terminator look. The Terminator was that guy, remember, who didn't know the meaning of the word 'defeat'. No matter how many times he was knocked down, he would haul himself up, dust himself off and come fighting right back at you.

When England played Sweden in the World Cup, Rose called the golfers who were not going to watch "wimps". But when push came to shove, and he was on top of the leaderboard, he saw the first 10 minutes then went to warm up before claiming the British Masters at Woburn. "I said sod the football," he laughs. "I had a chance to win a big one." Rose certainly has a sense of humour but he is also deadly serious.

To play against Tiger Woods would be good for my maturing process. I'd like to think I could give him a run for his money

The goose has landed

Two years ago, this South African golfer was an anonymous journeyman pro. Then he won the US Open, and this season he is attempting to be the European Tour's No.1 player for the third year in a row. The world has certainly heard of Retief Goosen now. But what makes him tick?

WORDS: **Jock Howard** PHOTOGRAPHY: **James Cheadle**

Behind the laid-back
exterior there lies
a focussed and
determined individual.

Shortly after Retief Goosen won the 2001 US Open, the South African President was on the phone. He was telling the man in question what an extraordinary thing he had just achieved. Goosen was on the other end of the line, saying it was no big deal and acting as though he had just won the monthly medal. On his way to the airport, Goosen's two IMG managers held the trophy more than he did. One of them thought it would be nice to hire a private jet to fly back to Britain. Retief poo-pooed the idea and said he would rather fly on a commercial airline. At the check-in desk, the IMG man said to the British Airways girl: "Do you know who this is? He has just won the US Open." Behind him, Goosen looked bashful and embarrassed. Shy, quiet, laid back and very modest; and – however many majors he wins in the future – that isn't going to change.

Retief Goosen is often referred to on tour as being 'as loose as a goose'. Look the term up in Brewers' Dictionary of Phrase and Fable and you will find the following: "Very relaxed; perfectly easy. The phrase owes as much to the rhyme as anything, but could also allude to the notion that a goose has loose bowels."

Aged 17 he was playing golf with his cousin, Henri Potgieter on their home course in Pietersburg, South Africa. He pushed his drive on the 7th hole into the trees and just before he reached his ball, a bolt of lightning struck the tree and flipped the Goose 15 feet through the air. His clothes were burned from his body, his shoes dissolved into his feet and his glasses were 30 yards away. His underpants and watch had melted to his body and the shafts of his clubs were welded together. He'd stopped breathing because he had swallowed his tongue. Yup, that would do it. That would make the insides a bit wobbly.

Joshing aside (and the man himself can laugh about it, mainly because he doesn't remember anything), Goosen is very lucky – now aged 33 – to still be alive. Indeed, if a doctor, playing in the group behind, had not pried his tongue out of his throat and administered CPR, he wouldn't be.

His mother, Annie, is not the only person who believes this incident changed him as a character and made him a bit more introverted. "He hasn't had the easiest of times growing up," says Gary Evans, who roomed with him for seven years when he first arrived on the European Tour. "I think when you've been through something like that, and then do military service, it teaches you to put things into perspective. At the end of the day, Retief appreciates that golf is just a game. It's not a life and death thing."

At first sight, Evans is a surprising friend and confidant of Goosen. Evans is the guy who went beserk after holing a putt on the penultimate hole of this year's Open and told his Mum – with the world watching – that he loved her. Goosen is the guy who is so shy and quiet he wouldn't say boo to a…well, to a web-footed bird like a large duck.

Goosen is so laid-back he is horizontal, not a bad attitude to adopt in a sport which, through its leisurely nature, can reach the most extraordinary heights of nail-biting tenseness. Pros like Sandy Lyle and Fred Couples won majors embracing such a posture. Maybe it's also a South African thing, because Ernie Els

> "Goosen didn't have the easiest of times growing up. But he was able to put things into perspective. He appreciates that golf is not a life or death thing...it's just a game"

Goosen's swing is a thing of beauty, one of the smoothest and effortless on the circuit. His medium and long-iron play is a match for anyone.

GETTY IMAGES

(aka the Big Easy) has a bit of 'loose' in him as well. So does the phenomenal tennis player, Pete Sampras. Goosen is also very shy. Indeed, before he met his wife, Tracy, who is from Kent, he was painfully so. Tracy has shown him a world away from fairways and greens. She was working in PR at the Belfry for the 1993 Ryder Cup when the Goose first met her, and everyone close to him says she has transformed his life. They got married a couple of years ago, at Leeds Castle in Kent. Two golfers came to the wedding – Michael Campbell and Gary Evans.

GETTY IMAGES

Retief from sand. "I put all my concentration into thinking about where I want the ball to finish."

Goosen has one of the most smooth and effortless swings on the circuit. It is a thing of beauty. When he is on song, his medium and long iron-play is a match for anyone. "When I'm actually swinging the club," he says, "I don't think about anything in the golf swing. I just put all my concentration into thinking about where I want to hit the golf ball and where I want the ball to finish. I don't think of any technical things during the swing. For me, it all happens a bit too quick to get into all that."

But we want more from our sports stars. It's not enough that they play superbly well. They must also entertain, be witty, nice, attractive, friendly, eloquent, kind to animals and so on.

The Goose is most of these things, but the one thing he is not is a brilliant interview. Very nice and polite but… Ask him what he bought with the $900,000 first prize cheque he got for winning the 2001 US Open and he will reply: "Nothing really." Ask him what he would like to see on his epitaph and he will say: "It's really up to other individuals how they want to remember me." Quiz him on his hobbies and he will smile softly. "I like watching sport on TV. Darts particularly."

(Actually, and apologies because this is a bit of a diversion, but the Goose is nuts about darts. Phil Taylor is one of his all-time heroes. "He's pretty much the greatest sportsman living in the UK. People don't realise that. He's won the World Championship 11 times in the last 13 years.")

Goosen's first language when he was growing up was Africaans rather than English. But just because he is not immediately forthcoming with people he doesn't know, does not mean he is dull and one-dimensional.

"It's true he's not the sort of guy who's going to dye his hair pink and streak naked down a beach," says Evans. "But he's just a really lovely chap. He enjoys his water-skiing, and going to the gym. He loves his cars and watching movies. The bottom line is he is a really nice, quiet and shy guy.

"I remember once I took him out in Germany. We'd both played really badly in the first two rounds. Retief doesn't really drink, and I took him for what I think was his first ever pint of Guinness. We were out late and at four in the morning I woke up to go to the toilet. My head was spinning a bit but I could still just make out this shadow in the corner being ill. Because Retief had never drunk much before, he wasn't used to it, and he was in a terrible way. We had a good chortle about it in the morning."

"I'm not going to go around making jokes like Lee Trevino," says Goosen. "Trevino felt comfortable playing golf that way. Others feel comfortable being serious and focusing on every shot."

The most extraordinary thing about Goosen's career is how

– so far – it has been a game of two halves. For the first 11 years of his professional life, he was a solid player, but nothing more. Then came Southern Hills in the summer of 2001. Two putts from 12 feet to win the US Open. Instead he took three, missing his second one from two feet. Missing short putts to win majors has often ended players' careers. It's a bit like being struck by lightning. You can't just jump up, dust yourself off, and get on with your life. Look at Doug Sanders who was never the same player after missing a tiddler at St Andrews in the 1970 Open. Or Scott Hoch, who still wakes up in the night screaming about his blunder in the 1989 Masters.

It took Goosen five minutes to recover from his miss. When he walked off the green, those around him couldn't look him in the eye for fear they had just seen a man destroyed. But he was incredibly composed and couldn't work out what all the fuss was about. It was testament to the sort of character he is. That's what makes him different from every other professional out there.

GETTY IMAGES

Becoming the best

So how did this man go from being a moderately good player to a great one virtually overnight? What was the catalyst which enabled him to jump from 85th in the world to 4th in a heartbeat?

Retief Goosen: "Very few players come straight in and win their first few majors. It's like Formula One. You've got to gain experience and learn how to play with your equipment, how to play in majors. Maybe I didn't quite believe I could do it. But then there is a point we all reach and there's nothing left to fear."

Jos Vanstiphout, his one-time coach: "He always had the talent, even at the start of his career. But he's a very introspective sort of guy and he just never quite realised just how good he was. Really. That was all it was. That's where I came in. I gave him the self-confidence to believe in himself."

Gary Evans, his long-time friend: "The final piece of the puzzle was his marriage to Tracy. She has been the most important part of the change in him. She's a lovely, outgoing person, and she has given him that final bit of self-assurance which he lacked."

Sealed with a kiss. Wife Tracy gave Goosen the last bit of self-assurance he needed.

The secret library that inspired 12 major victories

David Leadbetter opens the doors to reveal his unique collection of books that helped launch the careers of Nick Faldo, Ernie Els and Nick Price.

WORDS: STEVE CARR. **PHOTOGRAPHY:** BOB ATKINS

The swing guru at home in his study, Orlando, Florida, February 2002. He coached Nick Faldo to six major trophies, Nick Price to three, Ernie Els to two and Ian Baker-Finch to one.

BUTCH HARMON HASN'T played on tour since 1971, yet as a golf professional he's more famous than most of the current world top 20 players. It's not the marketable nickname that singles him out (if Butch and Tiger both used their real first names they would be Claude and Eldrick). It's not the fact that as a tour pro, the Vietnam veteran was prone to hot-headed, on-course tantrums (he doesn't like to talk about either subject). Nor is it that the history books record that his father, Claude senior, won the Masters in 1948 and was a close friend and teacher of the great Ben Hogan.

No, Butch Harmon is famous for one thing and one thing only: being Tiger Woods' coach.

The light that illuminates Tiger's stardom so brightly has reflected back onto the 59-year-old, making him an 'A list' celebrity in his own right. At tournaments, fans push past major winners Davis Love, Justin Leonard and David Toms to catch a glimpse of Butch. And even when he's working on the range with one of his other pupils – Darren Clarke, José Maria Olazábal or Mark Calcavecchia – it's the aura of Tiger that attracts the mesmerised stare of the masses.

In keeping with his celebrity status, Butch lives in Las Vegas. And while down the road Tom Jones performs nightly at the MGM Grand, Butch is the star of his own show at the Butch Harmon School of Golf at the glossy Rio Secco Club. For just $500 an hour, you can hire the number one coach in America for a lesson.

The academy building itself is a surprisingly modest affair and, although stuffed to the ceiling with high-tech cameras to capture the most intricate movements of the golf swing, the roll down doors of the driving bays give the place the feel of a mechanic's garage. Strange then that Butch should refer to his regular fine-tuning of Tiger's swing here as 'maintenance'.

But something of that Tiger magic sparkles all around. Gifts from Woods adorn the walls: 18th green flags from his major wins, golf bags, caps and signed photographs. There's more memorabilia in Butch's office, where we talk.

It's nine years since Tiger, then a ferocious young amateur capable of blasting the ball 40 yards further than he does now, was introduced to Butch. Harmon, who had just coached Greg Norman to Open Championship success, recalls the day clearly:

"It was August 23rd 1993 when he and his father came over. I was living in Houston, Texas, and the US Amateur was being played nearby.

"I'd heard about him, but I'd never seen him hit a shot. I still have the film on my computer. It was an unbelievable raw talent. It wasn't very polished, but he hit the ball ridiculous distances and had a wonderful short game. He didn't have a variety of shots, though – he just stood there and hit the ball as hard as he could. I said to him while he was practising drivers, 'When you get to a tight hole, all good players have an automatic shot where they absolutely have to drive it in the fairway. What do you do?' He said, 'I don't have one. I just aim down the middle and swing as hard as I can. I figure then I'll be close enough to the green to manufacture something.' I thought that was an arrogant little comment, but the more I got to know him the more I realised that was really his theory."

Earl Woods had brought his son to Harmon for a specific reason. Butch had had the guts to tell Greg Norman he had to change his swing to make it work under pressure. Having seen the potential in Tiger, Harmon was now keen to coach him too. But there were conditions.

"It was an interesting scenario because I lived in Texas and Tiger lived in California and we weren't really going to get to spend much time together," Harmon explains. "He was still in high school and they didn't have any money. So I told them two things: 'One, I won't charge you a dime until he turns pro and then I'll send you a bill (which I did, and it was a very hefty bill, but they had no problems paying it). And secondly, you've been your son's teacher and if we are going to do this it's not going to work if you are going to dispute everything I tell him to do.'

"Earl said, 'No problem,' and in nine years we've never had a problem. He's never interfered with anything I've said or done – he's been very supportive."

During those nine years, Butch and Tiger have focused on two goals – making Tiger a better player each year and winning major championships. In the first four years it was clear that Tiger was improving under Butch, but few expected him to win his first major, the 1997 Masters – and certainly not by a record 12 shots.

By then, his swing – wide, shorter than average but immensely powerful – looked like it would be a winner every time. But Butch and Tiger set about making it even better, to deliver greater consistency and control. This too they achieved and seven more major victories followed, including this year's Masters and US Open.

Now Woods and Harmon are working on delivering more accuracy into Tiger's iron game. It's this insatiable desire to improve, learn new shots and, specifically, win every major he plays in, that convinces Butch Harmon that there's more to come from Tiger Woods.

So what is it about this special relationship – professional and private – that has made Tiger Woods and Butch Harmon so successful?

LAUGHING GAME: Butch and Tiger enjoy a special relationship both off and on the course. Butch says they have had few, if any, disagreements in their nine years together.

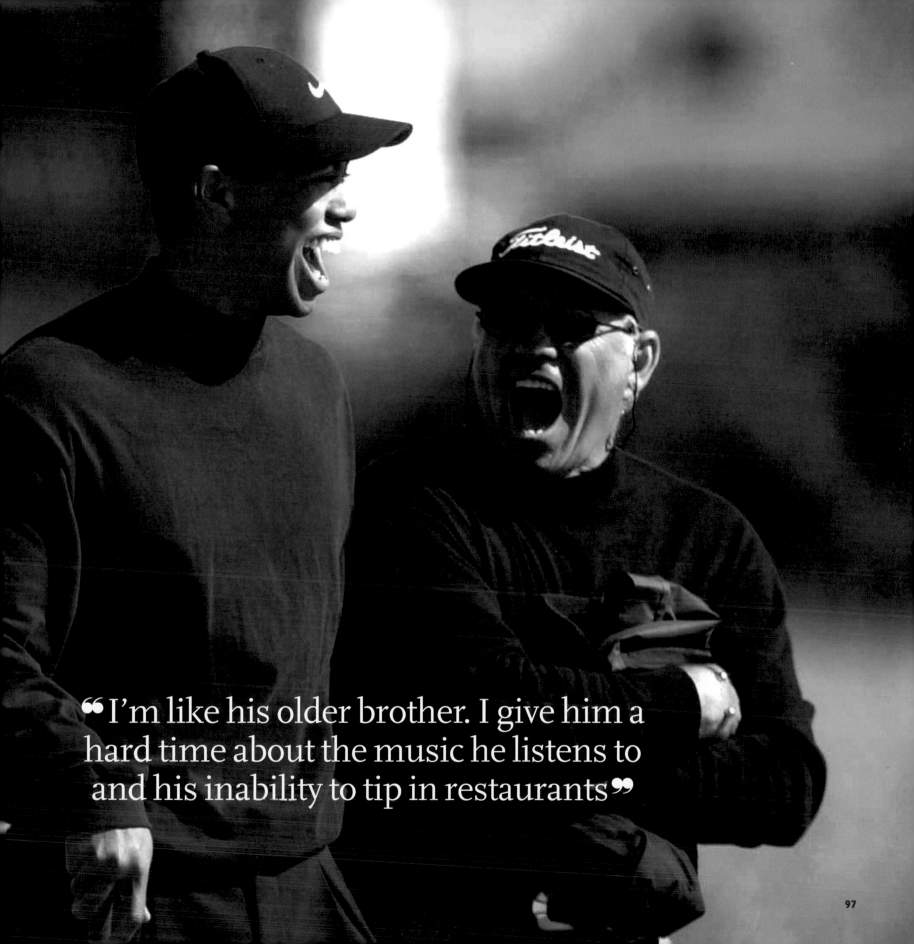

❝I'm like his older brother. I give him a hard time about the music he listens to and his inability to tip in restaurants❞

"Tiger trusts me and knows that when I tell him something I'm not guessing, but I've researched it and have watched hundreds of hours of film"

How would you describe your working relationship with Tiger – are you a team, or is he the master and you the servant?
I wouldn't say I am his servant. I think we're a team. The key to our relationship is the respect we have for each other. I have all the respect in the world for Tiger Woods. But he has a tremendous amount of respect and trust in me, too. He knows that when I tell him to do something I'm not guessing, but I've done my homework thoroughly and I understand why we should do things.

Does he put 100% trust in you?
Ultimately, with any player, it's their decision to listen to what you have to say. In Tiger's case he wants all the input you can give him.

Do you always get results with Tiger?
Most players you coach are limited in what they can do, but Tiger Woods is unique because he can do anything. Therein lies another problem, though, because you have to be sure when you are telling him what to do that you are 100% correct. It's funny, I get asked all the time if I ever thought I was going to screw him up? My answer is always that I never thought about it until a reporter first asked me.

So, have you made any mistakes along the way?
No, I wouldn't say so swing wise. Everything we've done has been part of a long term improvement plan. It's not just my plan, it's our plan and we discuss it together and work on it together. There's a reason for everything we do.

Have you ever disagreed about anything?
In all honesty, in nine years we've had very few disagreements.

That's highly unusual in a normal working relationship, don't you think?
I think it's very unusual. I'm not saying we've never had something we didn't both agree on, but there's never been an ugly interaction. Our relationship has always been very upfront, so if we ever have anything on our minds we're both man enough to look each other in the eye and say, 'Wait a minute, we need to talk about this.' And that's one of the reasons the relationship has worked so well.

There must have been times when you have told Tiger to do something and he hasn't felt it's right.
No, not really. Tiger soaks up knowledge like a sponge. He's always wanted to learn. To this day he wants to learn. I know that sounds unusual when you know how good he is and, when he's firing on all cylinders, how much better he is than everyone else, but he always wants to learn new shots and improve. We always talk at the end of the year, what the year was like, where we need to improve. Right now we're working on improving his accuracy.

When you say you have a plan and you review the year, does he actually write these things down?
He keeps everything in his memory. He's got great retention of the things

we've worked on in the past. It's funny, if I'm not at a tournament and he's played a poor day, I'll have seen him on TV and I'll call him and I'll say, 'What did you do?' He'll say, 'I went to the range and worked on this and that,' and I'll say, 'Oh, that's something new.' And he'll say, 'No, Butch – we did that about six years ago.'

How detailed is his knowledge of the golf swing?
Very detailed. He's interesting because we'll be at a tournament and you'll think he's not really watching anyone on the course, but we'll be on the practice ground afterwards and he'll say, 'Did you see that shot so and so hit, did you see how far they had the club on the inside?'

Which players' swings does he like?
He's always said he's never had a role model for his swing. He likes aspects of many swings – he liked the way Greg Norman drove the ball, he liked the way Ben Crenshaw putted and so on. He likes José Maria Olazábal's short game. I can remember him picking José Maria's brains a few years ago. He said to him: 'How did you play that shot, how did you put so much spin on it?' That's the other neat thing about Tiger – he will go up and ask players how they play a shot. And from a guy of his stature that is certainly very unusual.

How do players react when Tiger comes over to ask them how to play a shot?
They love it. José Maria loves Tiger. There's a mutual respect between José Maria and Tiger that is unbelievable. I think they're very similar, other than the fact that Tiger has a lot more natural ability than José. They're both warriors, they're like gladiators, they won't quit, they'll fight, they'll figure out a way when they don't have it.

Tiger told me after they played the third round at Augusta together this year (Olly played poorly on the front nine but came back and shot sub 32 on the back nine, while Tiger shot the easiest 66 you could ever imagine) that when they walked off the 18th green José Maria said, 'It's been a pleasure to watch you play today.' And that's a great compliment because most players would say, 'nice round,' and then go about their business. But that's what José Maria is like.

Describe the swing Tiger had when he first came to you?
When he was young, he wasn't physically strong. He had a long, loose swing that had a lot of hitting with the hands in it. As he got older and stronger, and as his technique changed, his swing became more efficient. He doesn't hit the ball anywhere near as far now – he could hit it 30-40 yards further before, but he had a hard time controlling it. But you see a swing now that is a lot more under control. It's much more mechanically sound as far as the positions are concerned. You see a swing now that can produce many more shots – and under pressure, too. When you build a golf swing it has to work on the back nine on a Sunday afternoon. And he's worked very hard to be consistent and create a motion that allows him to be repetitive under pressure. Now, he's had to get stronger to do that, which he's done, and he's now in perfect physical condition.

JOS VANSTIPHOUT

 GOLF WORLD   As originally published December 2002

Would you trust this chain-smoking, fast-talking former toilet cleaner and failed Belgian pop star?

Seven years ago no one in golf had ever heard of Jos Vanstiphout. Now he is a millionaire tax exile and his unique mind coaching has helped Ernie Els and Retief Goosen win the British and US Opens. Does he have a magic formula or is he massaging egos with words of the bleedin' obvious?

Words: **Derek Lawrenson** Photography: **Tom Howard**

A round with

GARY PLAYER

GOLF WORLD As originally published February 2001

Gary Player with Steve
Newell, Monte-Carlo GC,
October. He may have
travelled 12 million miles,
but on the greens, every
inch still counts.

The Entertainer

He's travelled 12 million miles to play golf. He's given a lesson to Elvis, still does a thousand sit-ups a day, and can't understand pros who refuse the chance to win money because they're 'too tired'. Steve Newell tees it up with Gary Player, and struggles to get a word in edgeways.

PHOTOGRAPHY: ANGUS MURRAY

THE TIME IS EIGHT O'CLOCK IN the morning. The place, Heathrow departure lounge, gate 26. I'm waiting for the man in black, a somewhat diminutive figure at 5ft 9in, but a true giant of the game: Gary Player, winner of golf's Grand Slam.

This particular rendezvous has taken 12 months to arrange, hardly surprising when you look at the man's punishing, globetrotting itinerary – he spends just 30-odd days a year in his own bed. But the waiting is finally over. Today, in the millionaire's playground that is Monte Carlo, I'm due to play against one of the greatest golfers who ever lived.

Gary arrives right on time. He is dressed in an immaculate blue blazer, black slacks, black polo shirt and polished black brogues. At 65, he is tanned and super-trim, as you would expect of someone who still does 1,000 sit-ups every day, and has distinguished platinum coloured streaks in his swept-back dark hair. He must be the healthiest-looking 'pensioner' in the world.

Player has come a long way from the poor boy who started out making a measly £30 a month as an assistant pro in the early 1950s, and who pocketed £100 for winning his first pro tournament in South Africa. A long way, indeed. Twelve million miles, in fact, which is his rough estimate of how far he's travelled in his near 50-year career as a tour pro. Twelve million miles! That's a trip to the moon and back, 25 times.

"I reckon I'm the most travelled human being on the planet," he says.

It's a mind-boggling statistic, but believable once you realise what he is like. I have never met a person who has such enthusiasm, such unquenchable get-up-and-go for golf and life.

"I love my life," he says. "I love people, I love golf. But it's been a hell of a sacrifice being away from home so much, being away from my children, my wife."

Dedication and hunger have driven him on. "I don't know whether you're born with it, or whether you cultivate it," he says. "But all I know is I've always had it. I always kept trying no matter what. I had determination to suc-

ceed, mainly I think because I was poor as a youngster. If you're poor and you struggle you're going to be hungry for success. That hunger has never left me."

He's got patience, too. Which is just as well.

The most glamorous golf location in Europe?

His arrival coincides with the announcement that our plane has a leaking water tank and will therefore not be taking to the skies any time soon. Gary shrugs his shoulders, raises an eyebrow and says: "What can you do?" in the manner of someone well accustomed to the tedium of airport delays.

As it happens, we do something that I couldn't have done unless I was travelling with a man like Gary Player – head straight into the First Class lounge. We sit there, seemingly a million miles from the usual airport hubbub, drinking tea, eating shortbread biscuits (I win that particular contest three and one, an omen perhaps for our game this afternoon?), reading

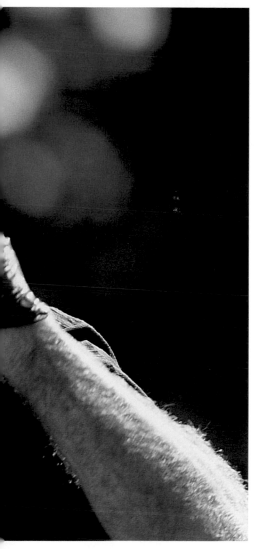

view. Equally he cannot get his head round the notion of players wanting to be paid to play for their country in the Ryder Cup: "They made out they wanted to give the money to charity," he says. "But they only said that after a lot of fuss was made."

It's not that Gary resents the vast sums of money being made today. He is, after all, a very rich man himself. But he worries about its effect on the game and, aside from that, doesn't seem to have lost sight of the value of a dollar.

He fixes me with one of his listen-very-carefully stares. "A friend of mine once gave me some very important advice about money. He said: 'Money's not the most important thing in life, but I still rank it up there with oxygen.'"

Gary ranks fitness pretty highly, too. People used to laugh at him when he came out on tour eating bananas on the golf course. Now everyone does it. Pre-Player, I doubt there was a single golfer who went to the gym. Now it's frowned upon if a top golfer does not. Even now he goes to the gym every day and he can still leg press 300lbs.

His sit-up regime gives him rock hard stomach muscles – I know, because during our round together he invites me to thump his stomach.

He enjoys good food, but certain things are a definite no-no. "Poison," as he calls them. He looks at Angus, our photographer on this assignment, and says: "If I offered you four tablespoons of fat in the morning, would you eat it?"

Hastily wiping the biscuit crumbs from his lips, Angus says he would obviously refuse. "Well why would you eat a bacon sandwich for breakfast then? It's bloody poison!"

After a two-hour wait our plane finally gets announced for boarding. Almost simultaneously there is a security alert and the alarms start going off, prompting a hasty evacuation of the First Class lounge. A woman travelling on her own, thoroughly flustered by the commotion, says to no one in particular: "What the hell's going on?"

Gary steps in. "Just finish your last few sips of tea and take your time. There's no need to panic," he says.

the papers and chatting about this and that. Lots of top sportsmen either talk solely about themselves or scarcely talk at all when journalists are within earshot. With Gary, however, you get a genuine two-way conversation.

He has forthright opinions on all things and becomes highly animated when we get onto the subject of the amount of money in golf these days.

"I read about golfers turning down the chance to win a million dollars because they're tired. Tired! How can a young man be tired? This is a million dollars we're talking about here. Am I mad? Is it just me?"

I remark that it isn't just him, and that most people in the street probably share a similar

GARY PLAYER ON...

Gary at Wentworth in the '60s. His divots are still flying 30 years on.

...the game of golf

"I think it's a game you can play forever, unlike other sports. In most sports, you have to retire at the age of 30; and in golf, you're just getting started. Everyone thought Jordan went a long time – he retired at 36; and Tiger Woods will hit his prime at 36."

"Anyone who criticises a golf course is like a person invited to a house for dinner who, on leaving, tells the host that the food was lousy."

Player's description of Carnoustie before the '75 Open.

"A good swamp, spoiled."

On what it takes to become a great golfer: "Patience, and courage would be the other one. Desire would be a big factor as well, and hard work. I've met very few people in my life with patience on the golf course."

"Everyone wants to be known as a great striker of the ball, for some reason. Nobody wants to be called a lucky, one-putting son of a bitch, and nobody thinks he is."

When Player won the Masters for the second time in 1974 he said, as he was helped into the Green Jacket by the defending champion Tommy Aaron: "I never seem to get one that fits."

Player first won the Masters in 1961 and took the jacket home with him to have it altered. This was against club rules, because traditionally all the green coats are kept under lock and key at the club. Player is the only champion to have one at his home. "I have the green coat in my closet. I didn't even ask them. If they want it back, they will have a helluva long way to travel to get it."

"Golf is not a game, it is a disease, a wonderful disease. It spreads out and gives jobs and pleasure to a lot of people."

As I discover on several occasions over the next two days, Gary has a special way with people. He greets all well-wishers and admirers with enthusiasm and warmth, as though he's been doing the fame thing for 40-odd minutes rather than 40-odd years. Everyone he comes into contact with walks away with a smile on their face. Gary says he loves people. On the evidence of this trip, people seem to love him too.

On the plane we go our separate ways, approxi-mately 40 rows of seats reflecting the economic chasm between a multi-millionaire sportsman and a *Golf World* journalist on a tight expense account. Unfortunately, the security alert has meant we've missed our slot for take off, and a further delay means the wheels eventually leave the tarmac three hours later than scheduled. By now I fear my long-awaited game with Gary will not happen this afternoon. Within an hour of arriving at Nice, I am certain of it.

We wait together at the baggage collection foyer, a tedious chore at the best of times but made worse on this particular occasion by the potentially awful con-sequences of a 'no show'.

I breathe a sigh of relief when Gary's clubs roll into view on the conveyor belt, shortly followed by mine. Half an hour later, though, the number of waiting passengers has dwindled to a handful, each of us growing ever more pessimistic about the chances of seeing our bags again. The conveyor belt then grinds to an ominous halt. The luggage has dried up. Gary's clothes have not arrived.

An elderly man approaches Gary to enquire where

Steve Newell
Age: 33
Amateur victories:
Nine (Barnet area)
Career highlights:
Two club
championships
Favourite colour:
White burgundy

Gary Player
Age: 65
**Professional
victories:** 163
(worldwide)
Career highlights:
Nine major
championships
Favourite colour:
Black

That power comes
from doing 1,000 sit-
ups a day. "I love
what working out
does for me," he says,
"but if there was a
pill that did the
same, I'd take it."

Player takes huge divots, and still
strikes his irons with the same major-
winning venom.

his own bags are. He evidently thinks the nine-time major winner is the luggage porter! Gary laughs and replies: "I'm not the porter, but I'm hoping to be promoted from floor sweeper quite soon."

Airport staff confirm, in that detached, not-my-problem kind of manner which they do so well, that Gary's clothes will hopefully be on a plane from London later this afternoon. We are then whisked away from Nice Airport in a black Mercedes, a professional security driver, appropriately and immaculately dressed in black, at the helm.

Gary is looking forward to meeting up with his wife Vivienne, who he hasn't seen in over a month. They are staying at the Hotel de Paris in Monte Carlo, right in the heart of Casino Square. Our hotel is less salubrious, a five-minute drive away. Gary gives me his telephone number.

"Ring me later," he says, "and we'll arrange a time to play tomorrow."

Later I discover that his luggage has indeed touched down in Nice, six hours after its owner. "Pick me up at 10am," Gary says.

The stage is set.

The morning of our showdown dawns bright, with clear blue sky. I arrive at the Hotel de Paris, punctual and raring to go. Inspired by the great man's influence, I have breakfasted on fresh fruit, muesli, orange juice and... okay then, I'll admit it, a large coffee and a Danish pastry.

Gary strides through the extravagant and spectacular reception area with a huge golf bag over his shoulder. Our driver offers to take his clubs off him, but Gary declines and skips down the steps of the hotel and puts his clubs into the boot.

Gary is again dressed all in black. Our driver is also dressed in black. My trousers are black, too. We look like we're off to a funeral – which with one false turn of a wheel on the spectacular but scary mountain road up to the golf course, we probably would be.

With one switchback bend after another and sheer drops to oblivion on one side, I think I would have preferred if Gary hadn't mentioned the fact that Princess Grace of Monaco was killed in a car crash on this very stretch of road.

The Monte Carlo Golf Club is surprisingly quiet – almost eerily so, given that the rich, the famous and the beautiful people will be here strutting their stuff in a matter of days for the start of the Monte Carlo Invitational, a sort of Pebble Beach pro-am for the European Seniors Tour. Come that time, people like me will be shot by the security guards.

In the locker room, Gary asks me how old I am. I say 33. How many majors had he won by that age?

"I'd won the Grand Slam by the time I was 29."

We make our way down to the practice ground. Gary has just got his hands on a new Taylor Made driver. His eyes light up as he tells me about the amount of extra carry he's getting through the air. Bashing balls to the farthest corner of the range, he can hardly tee them up quickly enough. He takes out another of his latest clubs, a Callaway 9-wood.

"It's amazing," he says. "I can hit it out of almost any lie and carry it 200 yards and it

GARY PLAYER ON...

PHIL SHELDON

Player with Nicklaus: They played not for money, but to be the best.

...other players

"In my first US Open ever, in 1958, I was paired with Hogan over the first 36 holes. He was a man of very, very few words, and I was sitting in the locker room when I felt a tap on my shoulder. It was Mr Hogan, and he looked at me with those eyes – they called him the Hawk because of that gaze – and said: 'Son, you're going to be a great player.' I nearly fell on the floor I was so surprised. He turned to go, and as he was leaving he asked: Do you practice hard? 'Yes,' I said, and he said: 'Double it.' Then he left."

"I hope the young guys don't get too greedy. They must not make money the main criterion. You look at players like Bobby Locke, Ben Hogan, Arnie Palmer and Jack Nicklaus and what they have achieved. They weren't driven by money, but an ambition to be the best. That is what matters."

"I feel sorry for Billy Casper. He can't putt a lick. He missed three 30 footers out there today."

"If Arnie asked all those people to go jump in the river, they would march straight over to the river and jump."

"I remember a fan once asked Tommy Armour: 'How can you miss a three-foot putt like that? I make them all the time'. This was at Winged Foot, and Armour bet him $5,000 that he couldn't do it that following morning. He wanted the man to have time to think what it's like putting for $5,000, something that we all know about out here. The man missed by four inches."

"For Tiger to beat Jack's record of 18 majors, that's a big task. He has the talent, but only time will tell. Tiger has as much ability as any man who ever held a club."

You wouldn't bet against Player getting down in two from here (he did). After a hole he'll hit some bunker shots for fun, nominating different styles – and pulling off every one.

Another one drops. "Nowadays the greens we play on are beautiful. In the early days they were nowhere near as good. Holing putts was tougher."

comes down like a wedge. I could never do that with a 3-iron, not even in my prime."

To prove the point, he treads a ball into the turf and absolutely flushes it, the ball almost knocking the 200-yard marker sign out of the ground.

"Not even Nicklaus could bring a long iron shot down from that height," he says.

On the tee Gary asks me what handicap I play off. Five, I reply.

"Is that five, as in five?" he says, "or five as in two or three?"

It's a genuine five. Gary knows I've played one of these matches against Ernie Els and wonders how many shots he gave me. When I tell him it was four, and that we played for £20 a side, he is incredulous.

"Four shots! You can tell Ernie from me that he must have deep pockets and short arms! I'm more than twice Ernie's age and I'll still give you five," he then says. "But if you're ahead after nine holes I'll reduce it to four."

The bet is 100 French francs. The nines on the course have been reversed for the forthcoming tournament, so our first hole is the par-5 10th. We both finish roughly 60 yards short of the green in two. My pitch is skinnier than Kate Moss, but it comes to rest six feet left of the flag.

"Oh no," cries Gary from across the fairway, "If I'm going to have to play against that sort of luck I'm in trouble!"

His pitch finishes ten feet past, which he holes for a birdie. I slot mine to match his birdie, but it's a shot hole so I go one up. Gary looks at Angus.

"I'm playing a crook," he says.

My tee shot at the par-3 next swiftly relieves him of that notion, a pulled 6-iron into a greenside bunker. Gary finds the green. As we get to our balls, Gary says to me: "I'll swap you."

I do a double take. Gary has a downhill 25-foot putt and I have a 60-foot bunker shot. And he wants to swap. This is a new twist to matchplay golf, and one I am happy to embrace. Gary then splashes his ball out of the bunker and across the green for a gimme. I trickle my putt down to four feet and miss. I've been had, by the king of matchplay!

Sand play is, of course, one of Gary's great strengths. In 1969 he went in 81 bunkers during the

Putting

"When it comes to putting, I've never worked on the same thing for long. I've chopped and changed all through my career. Back in the early days, the greens were so slow that your putting stroke needed to be very wristy, so you gave the ball a firm rap. Otherwise you'd never get it up to the hole.

"Let me tell you, the surface was nowhere near as good, which made holing putts a lot tougher. That's something no one ever seems to talk about when they compare golfers of different eras. Today the greens we play on are so beautiful, everyone's using a smoother, stiff-wristed stroke just to get the ball rolling. Forty years ago nobody putted like that, but now there isn't a single wristy putter."

Player wants to win everything, so nothing is left to chance... even for 100 French francs.

season and averaged getting down in two 79 times.

"I holed some and took three to get down on others," he says.

He hasn't lost his touch, either. Occasionally when we finish a hole he throws a few balls in the nearest bunker and hops in with his sand-wedge. He hits bunker shots for fun, nominating each one. "Low with spin," he'll say; "High with a soft landing." Each one is crafted perfectly to order. He threatens the hole from sand like the rest of us do with mid-range putts.

I'm surprised how far he hits the ball off the tee. He is unfeasibly flexible for a man of his age, a shining example of what keeping fit can do for you. His swing is long and flowing and he really gives it everything through the hitting area. On our third hole he hits a long, high draw, and when we get to our balls his is 15 yards past mine.

"Outdriven by a man twice your age," he says jokingly. "I bet you don't write about that in the feature."

He's keen to emphasise that long driving is just part of the game, though – and uses Tiger Woods to illustrate his point: "Everybody wants to talk about how far Tiger hits the ball. To hell with that! John Daly hits the ball a long way. Tiger is such a great chipper and

putter. He's got a great swing, but that isn't what makes him so good. He just has so much focus, he watches what he eats, looks after himself, practises hard.

"If anyone wants to beat him, they have to practise harder than Tiger, train more than Tiger, eat better than Tiger, basically try to outdo Tiger in every department. You can't do less and expect to beat him."

If Gary's early iron play is anything to go by, my prospects for winning the match look seriously iffy. The man's had 24 holes-in-one and he still hits his iron shots with venom, taking massive divots with his short irons. On our sixth hole he executes a purely struck 7-iron, the ball keeping low into the breeze and finishing three feet from the pin. Gary has suggested we play the 'inside the leather' rule for gimmes, but this putt doesn't quite qualify. It's too short to miss, though, and his third birdie of the round puts him 2-up.

Meanwhile I find myself on that well-worn path known as the 'bogey trail'. When I hook my tee shot on the next, Gary looks at my dejected expression and

WORDS: JOCK HOWARD
PHOTOGRAPHY: MIKE O'BRYON

A round with
TOM WATSON
GOLF WORLD As originally published August 2002

How does a man once rated the best player in the world, and who has won five Open Championships, two Green Jackets and a US Open, get in the right frame of mind to take on a 14-handicapper from Maybole Municipal?

It's elementary, my dear Watson

Not often do you get woken up by a phone call from an eight-time major champion. "Hello, it's Tom Watson here. I'll see you on the first tee at 12.30." For the first five minutes the only thing to do is fall back on your bed and pinch yourself hard in case you are dreaming. Once reality has been established, a dull sickness and tightening of the stomach muscles sets in as negative thoughts worm their way into your head.

Let's face it, if there is one thing guaranteed to make you choke on your Rice Krispies, it is the thought of playing golf with a man who won eight majors in as many years. In his prime, in the late 1970s and early 1980s, Tom Watson just had to turn up to make the legs of his opponents turn to jelly. The legs of this 14-handicapper were shaking so much it was very questionable whether he would be able to put on his golf shoes.

We were due to play a round at the very exclusive Tournament Players' Club at Heron's Bay, where they host the Honda Classic on the US Tour every March. It was a course Watson liked to practise on, partly because it was close to his Florida house, and partly because he knew he wouldn't get swamped by autograph hunters.

Only four men in the history of the game have won more majors than Tom Watson. Jack Nicklaus (18) Walter Hagen (11) Ben Hogan (9) and Gary Player (9) could theoretically tee it up with Watson and allow themselves not to feel a sense of inferiority; but that is not a luxury available to anyone else on the planet. To say I felt inferior would be to fall some way short of an accurate description.

"How good is your golf?" he asked, smiling as he arrived on the tee.

"Not great. I'm meant to play off 14. But the pressure of playing with a five-time Open Champion may mean I will crack."

"Listen Jock, I put my pants on the same way as you do."

"Are you sure you mean pants, Tom?"

"I'm sorry. You're right. I mean trousers."

There is a temptation to think of Tom Watson as an honorary Scotsman. Four of his five Open Championships came in Scotland. He loves fish and chips, British crowds and black pudding. But it is worth remembering he is actually the son of an insurance man from Kansas.

Watson stands for everything that is good about the game. He loves all the traditions and the history and was thrilled when he was recently made an honorary member

Up close and personal with an eight-time major champion.

"If the Open didn't exist I'd still come over and play your links courses"

Still one of the smartest and smoothest swingers in town.

of the Royal & Ancient Golf Club of St Andrews. He loves the purity of the links game, the challenge of it, the way imagination and weather become huge factors. He can't get enough of the vicissitudes of the weather in Scottish seaside spots like Carnoustie and Turnberry.

Given that we are playing on a course which is the antithesis of a Scottish links, a course which boasts alligators rather than pot bunkers and man-made lakes on 17 of its 18 holes, Watson looks a bit like a fish out of water.

You get the feeling that his freckled face and Huckleberry Fin good looks would look much more at home leaning into a stiff gale on the beach at North Berwick or sucking on a pint of Eighty Shillings with some caddies in The Jigger. When playing in Florida, in perfectly still conditions, in temperatures of 75 degrees, he reminds me of an SAS soldier who has been asked to forget all his training and do a touch of Morris dancing. That, however, doesn't stop him launching his first tee shot, straight as a

die, 280 yards down the fairway.

"One of the things I notice about getting older," says the man who will be 53 on September 4th, "is I am less good at reading the greens. Compared with the old days, my ability to decipher a golf course, to construct a game plan, has deteriorated. I am so dependent on yardage now that I don't really learn the golf course as much as I should. I guess its intellectual lazyness, but I've played professional golf for over 30 years now, so maybe I'm entitled to a bit of intellectual lazyness."

If this sounds like Watson is putting himself out to pasture, nothing could be further from the truth. Whisper it quietly, but the 52-year-old still thinks he can win a major championship.

"Let's put it this way, a lot depends on the golf course. If that sets up right for me, and if what I am trying to do with my putting works out this year, then I think I can win. On a hard, fast course I can win."

He is only playing three times on the regular tour this year with what he likes to call the "juniors". At the Masters he finished in a tie for 40th. Then in May, at the Colonial (site of his last US Tour victory in 1998) he finished 7th. His third outing will be at Muirfield, where he won his third Open in 1980.

Watson's love affair with links golf cannot be over-estimated and even when you are sitting in a caddie cart, in the middle of Florida, his mind keeps returning to places like Royal Dornoch and Muirfield. "I love the flavour of it. Before the Open this year, I'm going to play some links courses down in the south of England which I've never played before. If the Open didn't exist, I would still come over once a year to play your links courses."

Not that this was always so. On his first visit to a links course (Monifeith, two days before the 1975 Open at Carnoustie) he couldn't believe it when his drive at the third hole bisected the fairway, and yet bounced sideways and finished up against the face of a bunker.

"I didn't like it at all," he says. "Even when I won my second Open at Turnberry in 1977, I still didn't really like it. And I didn't enjoy the luck of the bounce at St Andrews in 1978. It really took me until 1979 at Lytham St Anne's.

"You have to come to terms with the fact that golf, a bit like life, is not intended to be fair. Bob Jones had to make the same adjustment. I wasn't conscious of a sudden decision; but that week I just told myself to quit fighting and join it. I tried to enjoy it. I suddenly realised that – as well as through the air – the game could be played along the ground. I tried to treat it like I did as a kid, when I couldn't hit the ball very far and I had to roll the ball up through the throat of the greens and play the bounce."

We had reached the fairway of the tricky par five 9th, and as if to reiterate Tom's point, I topped my approach with a 7-iron. It skittled along the ground but instead of visiting the throat of the green, dived instead into a greenside bunker. On the 11th, I got right under my tee shot, which took off like a rocket.

"The nose came down but the monkey died," says Watson enigmatically.

ALLSPORT

Tom Watson on his way to winning the 1977 Open at Turnberry using blade irons. Notice the lead tape on the back of the club to give added weight.

Why a traditionalist no longer plays blades

66 First of all, it's the look of my current clubs that I like. They are cavity-backed but they look like blades. I was with RAM for 20 years and when that company was sold, I looked at a lot of different equipment and companies. I went with Adams because I liked the people and felt they could make the equipment that I could use.

I met Barney Adams one year at the Phoenix Open. I was looking for a 3 and 4-wood which I could get in the air, and he provided me with Tight Lies clubs. Barney's personality had a lot to do with me signing. He believes in his golf clubs and he had a vision that we could make a difference in the market with the new GT graphite-tipped shaft. I believed in that and still do.

The graphite tip creates a little less vibration than a steel tip, but it can't be all graphite because the consistency of a steel shaft is much better. There are

inconsistences of distance with an all-graphite shaft, especially the shorter irons.

I had no problem with the irons and I put the driver straight in my bag. When I pick up a new club I judge it first of all on ball flight. It can't be too low or too high. It can't balloon. It can't dive.

The 353 driver has a very large head and is excellent. It is balanced beautifully. And the ball flight off it is better than any other driver Adams have produced for me. So, it was an easy transition. I'm not using the bi-matrix shaft in the driver – but I am in the 3, 4 and 5-woods because it is stable and I can control the ball very easily with it.

The most important thing with club design is the consistency of the clubhead, so that if you hit the ball in the centre, or the toe, or the heel, or the bottom, or the top – it goes the way you expect it to go, with every club. That

comes from the design. And that's why good companies like Adams shine, because they make a balanced clubhead.

It wasn't difficult to go from blades to cavity-backed irons. At first the feel was different, but we've tweaked the feel by going to a weaker shaft.

I played for about a year-and-a-half with a shaft that was a little bit too strong for me. And now, with a weaker shaft I'm getting that feel back which gives me a little bit softer hit.

When people are looking for a new set of clubs, I tell them the most important thing about an iron is how it sits on the ground. You have to have the lie sitting properly so that where the club hits the ground it should be right in the middle between heel and toe. In other words, you don't want your divots too toe-deep or too heel-deep. It should be square as it goes through. 99

It's time for players to use the same ball

66 Technological advances are essentially good news. The technological advances and innovation which have gone into racing cars have helped the efficiency of engines or the suspension systems of 'ordinary' cars. You're not going to drive a Formula One car in the street.

It's the same thing with golf clubs. And that line, between professional equipment and other equipment, is very fine. The problem has come with the ball. I think we should all play with the same ball. Now we have a golf ball that just goes a mile and that's very difficult to draw back from. It's within the framework of the Rules. We need to convince the R&A and the USGA to work with the manufacturers and say: 'All right, you know more about the technology and the aerodinamics of the golf ball than we do, so come on, let us reason together.' If you ask manufacturers if we have gone too far, for the most part they will say 'no'. But, I think there's enough common sense here to create a forum that discusses this in terms of trying to help the game.

The golf ball is the single most important reason the game has gotten easier. It doesn't curve as much. It goes straighter. It goes further. And it all is within the framework of the rules. But, on the other hand, the manufacturers are just trying to do a job. They are just trying to make a better golf ball. The bottom line is there has to be 'wiggle room' within the rules of golf. In other words some technological advances may be within the 'rules' but they may break what common sense dictates.

We need to have a forum between all the golf ball manufacturers, the USGA and the R&A. The rule makers have to make a case for one ball. And I'd be on their side if they did. 99

66 Watson would have won a bundle more tournaments if he hadn't suffered so much from the yips 99

"What does that mean?" I ask.

"I guess that's an archaic joke. It refers to the old NASA days when animals were sent up into orbit. You were too young to remember."

Unlike most golfers, Watson is very bright. He came out on tour with a degree in psychology from Stanford, and spoke out for George McGovern's candidacy for President which took some bottle given that his audience was made up of right-wing golfers. He has mellowed and become more philosophical over the years and yet is still very interested in politics. As we walk down the 13th fairway he tells me how he finds it extraordinary that the press still focus on whether or not the Al-Qaida terrorists should be referred to as prisoners of war. Much more important, he suggests, to focus on what they have perpetrated. He is a man of principle but also a terrific ambassador for the game he loves so much.

As he pushes a three-foot birdie putt to the right on the 13th I am reminded that putting has been Watson's Achilles heel since the early '90s. It is safe to say he would have won a bundle more tournaments (and possibly several more major championships) if he hadn't suffered so much from the 'yips'. In our round at Heron Bay he still looked like one of the finest strikers of the ball from tee to green. He shot four-under-par and didn't drop

a shot, but he still missed three putts from under five feet.

Lots of people have trouble putting. The difference with Watson is while others blame their equipment, their grip, their stance or their wife, he blames himself. I wanted to find out if his reluctance to use the broom-handled putter was a matter of principle for him.

"All I can tell you is it should be made illegal," he says. "That's a push. It's not a stroke. It should be banned. It is a push or a 'sclaff', – which according to the Rules of Golf – is not allowed. A 'sclaff' is in the Rules of Golf. It's an old term. I haven't used it because there are distance control problems on long putts."

At his worst, Watson found a three-foot downhill putt about as frightening and unnerving as if he had just spotted a rattlesnake in front of him. His nadir came in the 1996 Masters when, at the par three 16th, he hit a reasonable tee shot to within 45 feet of the flag, and then proceeded to five-putt. At the last Open Championship where he was in contention (1994 at Turnberry) he was in the lead with 11 holes to play, before three-putting the 8th and 9th.

Watson knows a lot about putting methods in the same way that an avalanche victim knows a lot about snow.

In the driving seat. Watson was in complete control of his Golf World challenge.

"Sam Snead used to do it croquet style and through his legs. A friend of mine, Jack Vickers, used to turn his back on the hole with short putts and look backwards at it. That is the only way he could hole anything.

"This year I am working on this new putting method. I used to twist my left wrist on the backstroke counter-clockwise, and that has caused me to miss it right. So, I'm trying to stop that twist. Because I haven't been doing it for very long, it feels as if I am going to miss everything right, like I did there. But I know if I do it for long enough, I won't miss it right. I've learned you have to practise a new habit for about three weeks before it becomes comfortable."

We shake hands on the 18th and as we walk to the clubhouse for something to eat, Watson says he is enjoying life on the Senior Tour but feels the new initiatives they have brought in this year (allowing fans into locker rooms and inside the ropes) may have gone a bit far. This year he has already been second three times and won over half-a-million dollars. What he really wants, though, is to win again on the main tour.

He orders a tuna salad sandwich on wholemeal bread, with lettuce, tomato and mayonnaise. When the waitress asks me if I would like fries with mine, Watson looks at her smiling. "Now, you've got to learn to ask him if he wants 'chips'; then he'll know what you are talking about." Once a Brit always a Brit.

Left - Guess who won the match?

Below - The Duel In The Sun (part two)

IN TOM WATSON'S BAG...

■ **Driver:** "Adams 363 GT brand new model. I play a little bit shorter driver than most people do – 44-inch shaft rather than 45."

■ **3-wood:** "This is my new 3-wood, the Adams Tight Lies GT. I play a 13-degree model which they call a 'strong' 3. It has a lightweight steel shaft with a graphite tip."

■ **Irons:** "These are the Adams Tight Lies Tour irons. They look like a blade but they are a cast club. This club has the GT shaft which is steel with a graphite tip, which eliminates some of the vibration of a mishit."

■ **Sand-wedge:** "Bevelled off towards the heel so I can lay it open, and that allows the leading edge to get down a little bit lower."

■ **Gap-wedge:** "In a tournament, as well as the sand-wedge, I'd carry a 'gap' wedge. This is a 52-degree wedge. I find it is a very good club from 115 to 100 yards for a full swing. To accommodate this, I will often take a 2-iron out. Both wedges are modelled on a club I used to play with years ago. I worked with Adams to produce this. It is a pear-shaped wedge with a slight offset. I like that particular look."

■ **Putter:** "I use a 278 Ping Pal (1978 model). This is actually a copy of the one I won quite a few events with at around that time. The putter I used got stolen from me and could never be recovered."

■ **Warm-up club:** "This is the club (left) I used to warm up with. It's an old weighted club. I like to swing it a couple of dozen times and it will get the juices flowing, get the cobwebs out."

A round with
TONY JACKLIN
GOLF WORLD As originally published September 2001

Firing into the deep blue yonder at Kungsangen's 6th, Jacko shows that he can still trade iron shots with the best.

Tony Jacklin

He is one of Britain's all-time sporting heroes, and the man who made the Ryder Cup the biggest event in golf. Steve Carr tees it up with Captain Fantastic – and finds that he's lost none of his old fire.

Photography: Angus Murray

As I amble up to Tony Jacklin on the putting green at Kungsangen GC near Stockholm, I can't help noticing his relaxed demeanour. On the eve of the STC Scandinavian International – one of his rare outings on the European Seniors Tour – Jacko seems comfortable with his lot in life as a gently ageing legend of British sport. Even his cream, chunky-knit, short-sleeved cardigan and greying temples give him an air of the father figure of British golf.

While I know that Tony's golf is far from the bristling game it was when he became a double major champion, it is still daunting to face a man who trailblazed for his country in the late '60s and early '70s. Not only was he the sole Brit to win the Open

Tony Jacklin
Age: 57.
Handicap: Scratch.
Captain: Europe's Ryder Cup team 1983, '85, '87, '89.
Famous for: Double major wins (1969 Open; 1970 US Open).

Steve Carr
Age: 35.
Handicap: 4.
Captain: Doncaster Under-13 mini rugby, 1978.
Famous for: Double chins.

Championship between Max Faulkner in 1951 and Sandy Lyle in 1985, he is still the only European US Open champion since Ted Ray in 1920. He belongs in the pantheon of great sporting Britons alongside Denis Compton, Stanley Matthews, Fred Perry and Steve Redgrave. So you might expect Jacklin to be threatening or aloof – but as we set off down the 1st in a blustery wind he seems almost oblivious to his standing within the game.

I spend most of the first two holes in the woods on the left, so it takes us until the 3rd to start chatting about the Ryder Cup. Already Tony has found out how Tom Lehman felt tackling a wayward Seve at Oak Hill in 1995, as I somehow up and down it twice from nowhere for halves. He

is unfazed by my good fortune – probably because of an association with golf's greatest matchplay event stretching back to 1967. Jacklin has seen it all before.

Actually though, while 1967 was the first time he played in the matches, 1957 – the year Great Britain & Ireland sneaked past the United States at Lindrick – was Jacko's Ryder Cup baptism. As a 12-handicap 13-year-old his father took him from their home in Scunthorpe to watch the tussle: "I remember touching Dai Rees' driver walking down the fairway, and he asked me to put a divot back. Ten years later he was my captain at the Champions' Club in Texas; it was a strange turnaround."

When Tony rolls in a birdie putt from 12 feet for a win at

What makes a good captain

"You have to be passionate about it. I put a lot of energy and thought in, and tried not to leave any stone unturned in terms of detail. With the pairings, I always tried to have the courage to do what I felt in my heart was the right thing. Sometimes you might get notions, and you must back those hunches.

"The worst thing to do is to walk into the team room and open it up to the floor. Sure, I bounced ideas off Seve – my man on the course – but ultimately it is the captain's decision.

"I think the cup is in good hands in Sam and Curtis. They have both had the pleasure and the pain of winning and losing, and know what it is all about."

**JACKLIN'S RECORD AS A CAPTAIN:
Played 4**

Won 2 Halved 1 Lost 1.

Man and boy: Tony's son Sean watches for any swing tips.

Maybe not as elegant as the old days, but mighty effective.

the 3rd, I begin to see what all the fuss was about those 30 years ago. With a twitchy breeze buffeting us on the short 4th, he strikes a pure 5-iron that barely grazes the turf to within a couple of paces, and sinks the slick left-to-righter without a hint of the anxiety that made him give up full-time golf in the 1980s. He confesses to his flaw after going 2-up: "I stopped when I was 40 because I got so anxious. I played from tee to green great but at times putted like a fool. It wasn't because I was a bad putter, just that I was so nervous. I just didn't enjoy it."

With the pressure off, Tony again looks like a man capable of stringing a few birdies together, but his ring rustiness lets me back in at the par-5 5th.

As we walk to the elevated tee at Kungsangen's 6th – a downhill par-3 over water – I ask him about how the emergence of the European team coincided with his reign of captaincy. I suggest that he catalysed the upturn in European fortunes. He is embarrassed enough to be put off his stroke, and flies the green with a 7-iron.

He talks about the problems before the golden years: "Back in the '50s and '60s there was a lot of bravado coming from the Britain & Ireland team, because I am

convinced they were in awe of the likes of Hogan and Snead. And because of my experience playing in the US, I thought I knew what had to be done. What inspired us was the feeling that the Americans had it all – we wanted to show that given a level playing field we had a chance.

"That's what I wanted to achieve as captain, to get the off-course things right – caddies travelling with us, creating a team room and so on. Getting those things right coincided with the arrival of the Seves, Faldos, Langers and Lyles *on* the course. It was perfect timing."

For once I also find perfect timing and strike my 8-iron close enough to tickle a birdie home, despite Tony pulling off an exquisite lob stone dead for a miracle save. Match all square.

Tony takes me back to the 1983 match at PGA National in Florida: "The press gave us no credence at all – most went off to Disney World and came back with Mickey Mouse bags. Yet it looked like us to win all day Sunday until Lanny Wadkins hit that wedge at 18. But there was wonderful camaraderie. We could sense that things were gelling – it was a fantastic effort and a

Tony's chipping dazzled all the way round – here he lands it on a sixpence to finish pinside at 6.

stepping stone. In 1985 we talked about going close last time. We sensed, given home advantage, that we could win."

Such is Tony's passion for Ryder Cup, and fascination with its history, that he has even commissioned a set of limited edition Ryder Cup furniture – some crafted by Lord Linley – with the centrepiece being a reproduction of Sam Ryder's old desk, which he bought to use himself in 1989. I put his slightly wayward approach shot at the 7th down to the waves of nostalgia washing over him, and manage to capitalise with another surprising birdie.

I come quickly back to earth at the 8th, however, when I flounder among the granite outcrops, and the match returns to parity. Just as my run reaches an abrupt end, one of a different kind starts for Tony as he sprints towards the nearest portaloo. Even at age 57, he shows the fleet of foot of a desperate man.

A few minutes later he trots back, and his new found freedom of swing nails one down the par-5. I watch his action intently. With a squat but rock solid stance, he is one of the old school as he turns and

thumps. It is his hand-eye coordination mixed with bricklayer's forearms and cyclist's thighs that power the ball away. No frills, no nonsense – just natural ability rolled into a mighty meatball. He comfortably reaches the 513-yard hole in two but zooms through the back, letting me in for another sneaky birdie and a one-hole lead through the turn.

As he pops another delightful lob stiff at the 11th – his secret is to keep his left hand and clubface going through together – Tony talks about the wonders of team golf: "Individual wins are purely selfish pursuits, but there are so many people involved with a Ryder Cup that winning one is very special. Don't get me wrong, I felt marvellous after my Open wins – but the Ryder Cup is somehow beyond that.

"The last thing I said before I left as captain was: 'Whatever you do, don't change the format'. To me it's a great format that probably favours the underdog, because you are not showing all your cards before Sunday. That almost guarantees a close contest."

The hit-and-run matchplay we are playing also favours the underdog, thankfully, and I stay 1-up

Left a bit, right a bit...

Steve Carr and friend talk their way round.

Still standing: The only European US Open winner in 82 years.

"The press gave us no hope at all in 1983. Most of them went off to Disney World and came back with Mickey Mouse bags."

thanks to another weapon up my sleeve. In 1971 Jacklin was turned over at the last in the final morning's singles by motormouth Lee Trevino, and inadvertently my Ryder Cup inquisition seems to break Tony's concentration enough for me to sneak one ahead with one to play.

To me this is a pressure moment – but not in the least bit to Tony. He has experienced one of the most extreme situations ever seen in golf. In 1969 he and Jack Nicklaus were the last singles out on the course with the outcome of the Ryder Cup hingeing on their game. Jacklin had just lost 16 to go 1-down and the tension was furious:

"The pressure was enormous, because you put yourself last," he recalls. "The team comes first. I knew the score better than anyone else. Everyone on 18 who heard the roar from 17, where I'd holed for eagle, thought I'd won my match, but they didn't know I had lost 16.

"You don't want to be where Jack and I were that day. I walked down the hill on 18 having hit 3-wood, and he hollered at me: 'Tony, are you nervous?' I said: 'Nervous? I'm petrified.' And he replied: 'I thought I'd ask, because if it's any consolation I feel exactly the same as you do.'"

Kungsangen Golf Club
STC SCANDINAVIAN INTERNATIONAL

Date: July 12th 2001

PLAYER A   **TONY JACKLIN**
PLAYER B   **STEVE CARR**

SENIORS TOUR CHAMPIONSHIPS
Scandinavian International

Hole	Yards	Par	A	B	Match
1	355	4	4	4	a/s
2	367	4	4	4	a/s
3	380	4	3	4	-1
4	168	3	2	3	-2
5	433	5	6	5	-1
6	174	3	3	2	a/s
7	382	4	5	3	+1
8	379	4	4	6	a/s
9	513	5	6	4	+1
Out	**3,151**	**36**	**37**	**35**	
10	392	4	4	4	+1
11	392	4	4	4	+1
12	185	3	3	5	a/s
13	428	4	5	4	+1
14	418	4	6	6	+1
15	279	4	4	5	a/s
16	156	3	3	3	a/s
17	495	5	5	4	+1
18	426	4	4	5	a/s
In	**3,171**	**35**	**38**	**40**	
Out	**3,151**	**36**	**37**	**35**	
TOTAL	**6,322**	**71**	**75**	**75**	

The Nicklaus concession in '69

"It was two feet – not three or four as some have said, but two. Was I pleased that he gave it to me? Relieved would be a better word!

"Could it happen today? I think yes. Jack and I were friends, our wives were friends, we fished together, we were pals. I was one of the few to go to America and play, but now many do, so friendships have been struck.

"I will tell you, though, that while it was a sporting gesture between friends, some of the Americans weren't so happy. There were some mean-spirited guys on that team in '69. Sam Snead was captain then, and he is a hard man. It didn't go down as well with Jack's team-mates as it did with everyone else."

Birkdale revisited – only this time it wasn't so important!

JACKLIN'S RECORD AS A PLAYER: Played 7 Won 13 Halved 8 Lost 14. Points: 17 (49%).

An honourable half between gentlemen (well, one of them anyway).

The valve was loosened and the streams of relief burst out when Jack conceded 'that putt' for a half and a tie.

Before we take on our 18th – a brute of 426 yards uphill and into the wind – Tony's charming nine-year-old son Sean shows us how the Jacklin legend might live on. Barely bigger than the bag he has been pulling for 17 holes, Sean stands up on the tee with his dad's driver and swings majestically at the ball, which rockets away to just shy of the 200 yard mark. We laugh. What price a Jacklin playing at Medinah in the 2011 Ryder Cup?

"He's got it all this kid I tell you," coos Dad.

But this hole more than any other today proves to me what talent still lurks beneath Jacklin Senior's fatherly exterior. A rasping drive down the middle is followed by a world-class 3-iron that, if transplanted to the wilds of a links, would have the galleries in raptures. All that's left is for Tony to coax his first putt to the brink of the hole. And although the second putt is truly unmissable, I can't help but pick it up and concede the halved match *à la* Nicklaus.

It has hardly been a battle in the mould of a Ryder Cup Sunday, but I feel delight and relief to come out with a half, just like Jack

Nicklaus did 32 years ago. Tony puts our day and the forthcoming Ryder Cup into perspective: "As long as it is a great contest conducted by gentlemen, where on the 1st tee you look your opponent in the eye and keep the games as sportsmanlike as possible, it doesn't matter who wins." Amen to that.

I've enjoyed Jacko's company greatly, and although some have found him a little too outspoken and self-congratulatory at times, I find him nothing but one of those 'gentlemen' he referred to. He is honest, and any slight immodesty is born from a genuine boyish pleasure about what he has achieved in the game.

And let's face it, Jacklin has much to shout about. We should be grateful for his achievements and his amazing input into the success of the Ryder Cup.

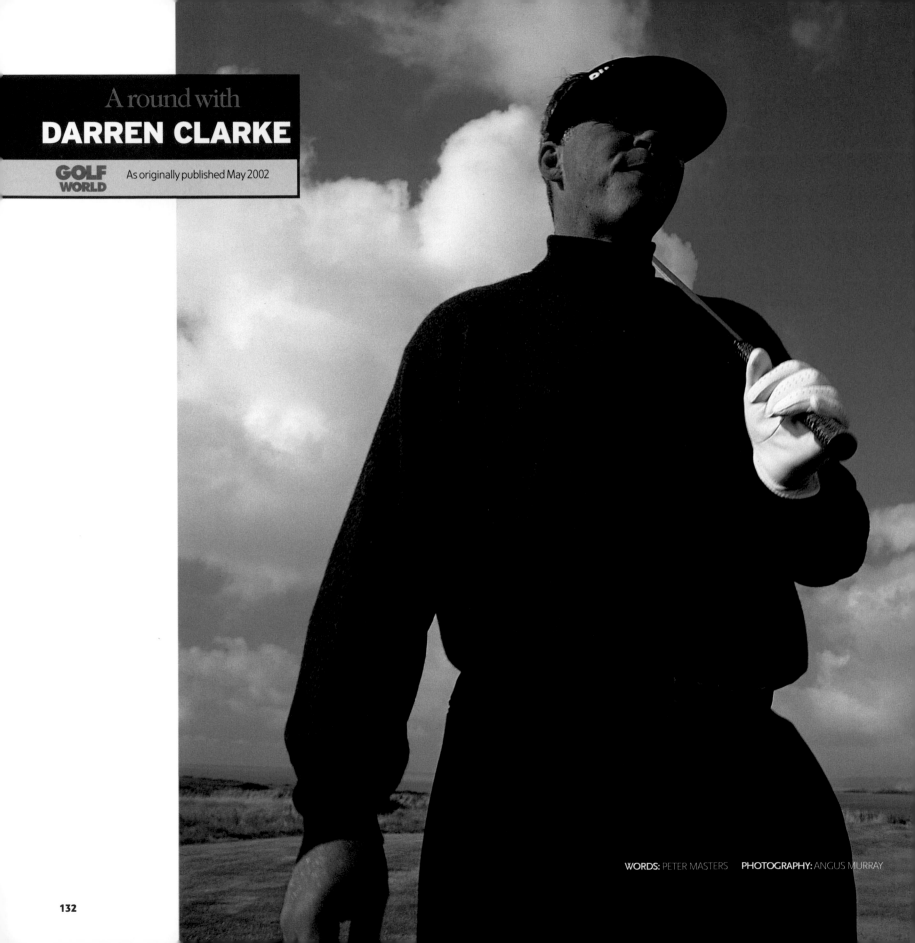

A round with
DARREN CLARKE

GOLF WORLD   As originally published May 2002

WORDS: PETER MASTERS   PHOTOGRAPHY: ANGUS MURRAY

132

Darren Clarke's Little Black Book

This is the true story of a thirtysomething Irish golfer and what happens if you find yourself added to his blacklist. It's a tale of gambling, matchplay and revenge. A dark sequel to Bridget Jones's Diary. Sort of.

Darren Clarke bears grudges. He has, in his mind's eye, a little black book into which he puts the names of those who have rubbed him up the wrong way. And there is no way out of it. Darren will, if it takes him weeks, months or years, eke out revenge.

One such unlucky candidate was a former sports writer for The Sunday Times who had the temerity to refer to Clarke as a 36-handicapper. This reporter rather laid into the Irishman after he had let slip a winning lead over Sergio Garcia in a match that cost Ireland a Dunhill Cup victory against Spain. "I hit it heavy from 64 yards on 18 and left it short of the green. Sergio beat me by one and I had cost Ireland the result. I took it bad," is about the gist of it for Darren.

He took the reporter's jibes even worse and sought retribution in a press conference at the Dubai Desert Classic months later when the media were waiting to question him about his triumph over Tiger Woods in the La Costa Match Play. Clarke pointed at the culprit and made him leave the room before he agreed to continue.

But did he think he was right to treat fire with fire? "Yes. And I'd do exactly the same again," he confirms. "I'm in the public arena and, yes, I understand that not all press will be good press, but it has to be fair criticism. You can't have someone playing off 18 or 20 calling me a 36-handicapper. This guy had no idea what I was trying to achieve with that shot."

For Darren Clarke, revenge is sweet. He says there are plenty in his black book and he is happy to wait until the time is right to deal with them. The black book is clearly not a good place to be and I just hope what I'm about to tell you doesn't constitute an invitation for membership.

It was three hours before our Golf World challenge match and the sun had just risen over the Irish Sea, bathing the links at Castletown, Isle of Man, in a yellow glow. Both of us were in our rooms and both were in bed, but the difference was, I was getting out and Darren was getting in.

Crashing out at six in the morning, after a night on the tiles at the casino in Douglastown hardly constitutes ideal preparation for our 9-hole showdown.

But then again you wouldn't have known it. I expected a groggy, big bear attitude on the 1st tee, but instead got a sparkling smile and cheery Irish repartee. This guy can party. Four sausages and three eggs might have had something to do with it, but he then drilled a 3-wood up the hill and over the back of the green on the par four opener. Darren Clarke lives life to the full and for that he should be applauded.

As we sauntered up the fairway, I asked him if the evening had been a profitable one – he had woken with a pocket stuffed full of crisp orange bills, but he couldn't remember whether they had been winnings or a loan from Chubby Chandler, his manager.

All our man can do is watch and suck his thumb.

Bet you can't get up and down in two shots. Oh dear!

❝Clarke kept thundering his drives and sizzling his iron shots. It was

"You like a bit of a gamble, don't you?"

"Yeah, I like a gamble."

"How careful are you?"

Darren paused a moment, looked me in the eye and said in a slow and deliberate manner, "Not very, at all!"

"Isn't there a danger of you becoming a bit of a gambling nut?"

"No, I wouldn't say that."

"So you limit yourself?"

"No, I wouldn't say that either."

"Have you ever blown a lot?"

"Oh yeah, oh yeah, definitely."

"What's a lot then?"

"A lot."

"Six figures?"

"A lot, a lot, a lot." The words tumbled out of Darren's mouth like an Irish chained melody. "I'll not say, but a lot. Shirt numbers, multi-corners, goal minutes – I'll bet on anything.

"At home during the winter, if the football's on television and I don't

man against amoeba. Windswept links are rather up his street"

support either team, then I'll have a bet to make it more interesting."

We reached my ball. I had a short pitch to the green.

"You don't want to use that," said Darren pointing to my sand wedge. "You need a 9-iron, then you can pitch it short and run it up."

But I'd been practising with my sand wedge in the back garden and gave my opponent such a non-plussed expression that he took pity and motioned me to continue.

The ball arced into the air, landed on the front edge, skipped along and dived into the hole. I screamed, but it was not my voice I heard, but

Darren's, because he was screaming too – and louder. He threw his club down in mock defeat and our palms came together in a resounding high five.

I was one up after one against a player whose achievements I should like to list in full detail immediately, but won't in the interests of space.

As a match, my fortunes went rather downhill from there. Darren had me widening my stance so I felt like I was straddling a horse and as I disintegrated, he kept thundering his drives and sizzling his iron shots. It was man against amoeba. Windswept links are rather up Darren's street.

Clarke unveils his new disco dancing pre-shot routine.

The perfect draw

Nowadays a perfect draw for Nick Faldo appears more on his design plans than it does on the golf course. The question is does that bother him? To find the answer we challenged the six-time major winner to a round of golf.

WORDS: PETER MASTERS PHOTOGRAPHY: MATTHEW HARRIS

Oblivious to the sea of sand ahead, Faldo's iron play is as crisp as ever.

Meet the two contestants

Nick Faldo
Age: 44.
Major titles: Six
(three Opens, three Masters).
Flying experience:
Helicopters.

Peter Masters
Age: 38.
Major titles: One
(World Ice Golf Champion).
Flying experience: Kites.

O F ALL THE ITEMS YOU MIGHT expect to see in a pro shop, the little metal train was not one of them. It sat on an imaginary track which circled a stand for Shadow Ridge-logoed polo shirts. It had a silver engine the size of two sugar cubes and behind it there were four little carriages in tow.

The relevance of such a trinket was not obvious until you moved closer to see a $75 price tag and the letters F-A-L-D-O engraved on the side of each piece. Britain's best-ever golfer has made a sizable impact in this Californian neighbourhood, so much so that it seems that anything with his name on it might seduce a prospective purchaser.

Nick Faldo is the talk of the town in Palm Desert, which is saying something when you consider that, as a golf course designer, he is up against such luminaries as Arnold Palmer and Jack Nicklaus. His new course, his first in America, has opened to rave reviews, and the buzz of excitement in the pro shop was becoming more pronounced as his arrival became more imminent.

This whistle-stop visit was to achieve three things: introduce Shadow Ridge to the American press; make some final adjustments to the course; and play golf with a journalist from the UK, namely me.

The first of those objectives was achieved in a tent on the practice ground, the other two were completed in unison, allowing a unique insight into the way a designer analyses the strategic subtleties of a golf course.

A sea change has occurred in Nick Faldo. He has got married for a third time, he has moved into a house in Windsor and the chapters of his future biography, the ones that include heroic tales of triumphs in golf's major championships, have all been written.

"I have rising damp, woodworm and a leaky roof, but lots of character," he says, referring to his new abode, although you mightn't have known it.

What is noticeable about his attitude is that it has become more relaxed and more open to those around him. He is a friendlier Faldo, a more honest and attentive one. He has also become reflective where he was once resolute.

We teed off. Nick, after a 20-hour flight and a couple of hours in a car, nailed it down the middle. I, after a relaxed breakfast and a bucket of balls on the practice ground, knobbled a heely one.

"I've been on the road 27 years and I've been shocked at how little time I actually get to myself," he ponders as we walk down the fairway. "Out of 52 weeks it doesn't feel good when I have only six spare. I want to start seeing friends. Sometimes it's embarrassing because they ring you up to suggest getting together and you have to say, 'Yes I'd love to, call me in six months'."

Friendship is something Faldo values far more now than he ever did in the past. As a pro golfer in an obsessional quest for major championships, making friends came well down the priority list.

Fall-off areas around the greens are a Faldo favourite.

Shadow Ridge is something different, or at least it is in comparison to the other courses in Palm Springs. This is why it has made such a huge impact. The story goes that in the first meeting between Faldo and his team, both parties threw down the same magazine, opened it at the same page and pointed to the same picture as a basis for the design. It was Kingston Heath in Australia.

As the round continues, you can tell by the way Nick surveys the terrain that this is a course that pleases him. As he points out a small blemish to his designer or explains the need for lethal drop-off points to me, he does so with equally enthusiastic relish.

The bunkering here is a work of art. Inspired by the great Alister Mackenzie, there is no symmetry to them, they twist and turn with the land, forming deep pits that are placed maddeningly close to the golfer's ideal line. So vertical and clean are the edges that they create shadows even when the sun is reaching the pinnacle of its route across the sky, hence the name Shadow Ridge.

His mind on the fine detail of the humps and hollows ahead, Nick's game looks as solid as it ever was. He probably doesn't know it, but he has parred the first handful of holes. It is time perhaps to draw him out of his designer cocoon.

"It all looks so easy, but when I watch you on tour it seems that you are trying too hard," I suggest.

"Well, it will look like that. When you are playing

"I thought it was all about getting my name on trophies, not getting people to think, 'what a nice chap he is'. I feel the impression of me was wrong. It was never created, it was purely out of the driven pursuit of trying to be the best. It would be really nice over the next few years to show that I have a different side."

FALDO'S DESIGN CV

Since Chart Hills opened for business in Kent eight years ago, Nick Faldo has added a further 11 courses to his portfolio. The majority of these are in Asia, but the Faldo Design group are now spreading the net much wider. A second course has just opened in America and there are further projects in Europe and Australia.

THE COURSES
● **Chart Hills**, Kent, England.
● **Faldo Course at Sporting Club Berlin**, Berlin, Germany.
● **Marriott's Shadow Ridge** Palm Desert, California.
● **Faldo Course at Wildfire** Phoenix, Arizona.
● **Faldo Stadium Course** at Mission Hills Shenzhen, Hong Kong.
● **Faldo Course at Eagle Ridge**, General Trias, The Philippines.
● **Ocean Dunes**, Phan Thiet. Vietnam.
● **Great Lake**, Rayong, Thailand.
● **Century Ban Chang**. Thailand.
● **Cikarang**, nr Jakarta, Indonesia.
● **Wuhan International**, Wuhan, China.
● **Royal Orchid**, Shunde City, China.

Design projects in progress:
Portugal, Greece, Connecticut, Mexico, Canada, China, Australia, New Caledonia and The Dominican Republic.

A round with
GARY ORR
GOLF WORLD As originally published March 2002

Putting his Orr in

WHAT YOU WILL LEARN
- How a pre-shot routine can get you in the groove for more consistent shots.
- Why you should make your practice sessions as realistic as possible.
- When it's worth sacrificing distance for accuracy off the tee.

GARY ORR
Coach: David Leadbetter.
Amateur record: Scottish International 1984-86.
Secret weapon: Kasco 2K 4-wood.
Course records: 62, British Masters, Woburn 2000.
Putting style: Leaves a gap between ball and putter.

STEVE NEWELL
Coach: National Express.
Amateur record: Club champion on two occasions.
Secret weapon: Talking too much.
Course record: 77 (briefly), Burhill Golf Club 2001.
Putting style: Leaves a gap between ball and hole.

This Scottish exile may lack the X-factor that separates Tiger from the chasing pack but hard graft and not a little talent has bagged him two tour victories and £2 million. Be inspired by Gary Orr's down to earth and realistic work ethic.

Words: Steve Newell.
Photography: Angus Murray.

Gary Orr is one of those highly professional, diligent characters who leaves no stone unturned in his pursuit of excellence. He knows his strengths and plays to them; recognises weaknesses and calls on both mind and body to eliminate them. The 35-year-old Scot considers course management and mental strength to be two of his greatest assets.

This was the first game ever to be played on the New Course at Burhill Golf Club in Surrey. Just how new is new? Well, striding out onto the virgin, vibrant green turf, there aren't even any tee markers in place. Which might explain why I then, ahem, proceed to tee my ball up on the practice chipping green. Oh, c'mon! It's right next to the 1st tee, honestly it is. Could've happened to anyone. Not the sort of mental aberration Gary is used to seeing. He is clearly amused.

Gary grew up not far from Loch Lomond and was a Scottish amateur international in the 1980s. Soon after turning professional he went down to Burhill to work as an assistant pro.

"I wasn't sure if I was going to make it or not, so I thought this was the best thing to do," he says. "That way I would gain experience and then get qualified as a PGA professional, which would be something I could fall back on if things didn't work out on tour."

A good plan, but not necessary. Gary secured his playing rights for the 1993 season and, swelled with sponsorship from a syndicate of 43 Burhill members, went merrily on his way to seek fame and fortune on the European Tour. In his first year he banked nearly £200,000 which was good enough to claim the Rookie of the Year title.

"As a rookie tour professional you're never quite sure what the standard is like and how tough the courses are going to be, or even whether you'll measure up," admits Gary. "But I kept my card easily and it gave me the confidence to go on."

Since then he has played in three consecutive Dunhill

Quick, while he's not looking. Golf World's Steve Newell gives his trusty 1-iron the full treatment as Gary Orr poses for the camera.

Cup teams for Scotland and in 2000 had his best ever season, winning the Portuguese Open and the British Masters at Woburn. His career prize money has sailed past £2 million. But our game comes hot on the heels of an enforced layoff due to serious food poisoning and a kidney stones illness. He looks fighting fit now, but it would be no surprise if his game was a little rusty.

Gary thumps his opening drive down the middle – a low and drawing flight ensuring the ball hugs the inside corner of the dogleg to finish in perfect position. He lofts a crisp mid-iron into the heart of

the green and cosies the ball up to 10 inches for an easy par.

Gary fires his drives low and his irons very high, which no doubt is a tasty combination when you're trying to seek out tight pin positions on tournament courses. His swing isn't what you, or even Gary, would call classic. But it gets the job done, which is more important than aesthetics. He makes a methodical, compact backswing and then zips through the ball with fast-hands.

One of the first things you notice about his game is that his feet are very square at address. They point

"I set myself goals at the start of each year. If I force my way into the world's top 50 that'll get me a start at Augusta, and I want to play in as many majors as possible"
Gary Orr

146

straight out in front of him, rather than slightly splayed as with pretty much every other tour pro.

"I've seem myself on video and it does look a little unusual," admits Gary. "But I tried to turn my feet out at address and it just felt uncomfortable, so I've kept it that way." Gary's long game is pretty dependable. It always has been, he tells me.

But what has really improved is his short game. On the 2nd he plays a 30-yard chip-and-run to two feet and on the 4th, he chips again – only this time with maximum loft – over a bunker to 12 inches. He says the key is to keep the technique basically the same and let the loft on a variety of clubs do the work for you. "What a lot of people don't realise," says Gary, "is that David Leadbetter (whom Gary works with, along with his associate David Whelan) is a really good short game coach, so that side of my game has improved over the last few years."

What he has also learned is the importance of patience. "One of the things you learn early on is not to 'short side' yourself. If there's a tight flag position, and there are plenty on tour, it's always in your mind never to miss the green on the same side as the flag because that leaves you the toughest recovery shot to save par."

Smart club selection, too, is part of course management and Gary has a secret weapon. Many times on the front nine he wields a small-headed lofted wood, punching a powerful shot out of light rough into the heart of the green on a par five and placing perfect tee shots into prime position on tight par fours. It has become a worthy substitute for the largely unloved 1-iron. "Not many tour pros use a 1-iron anymore," says Gary. "They're just so tough to hit. It's okay if you're teeing it up, but once you get in a little bit of rough

it's a total waste of time. These little 4-woods do the same job of a 1-iron and they're so much easier to hit; you can also use them out of rough and get them to fly high and land softly."

In the face of such logic I have a sudden and overwhelming urge to place a towel over the 1-iron that is poking its skinny little head out of my golf bag.

Gary plots a trouble-free route to a two under par 70 around this 7,000-yard layout, executing shots with a skill and efficiency that goes largely unrewarded on the greens. My untidy 77 was at least a course record – for all of 30 seconds.

Gary has worked hard to get his game to the stage it's at now – and is fully intent on working harder to get to the next level. Sure, he knows he has a secure and dependable career in golf, but at the same time he's desperate not to become merely a plodder. "I think you've always got to be looking at areas of your game where there's room for improvement and keep working on them," he says. "I set goals at the start of each year, but at the same time I try not to think too far ahead. Right now, if I get into the world's top-50 that'll get me a start at Augusta next year. I want to play in as many majors as possible." Where, of course, he'll come up against Tiger.

Some golfers are tired of being asked about Tiger, but not Gary. "I've never heard another player say a bad word about him," says Gary, "which is incredible. He handles himself amazingly well considering the pressure he's under. He's great for golf, all the other pros are going to benefit from him because if you play well the rewards are just so much greater now. I think just being around at the same time as him is pretty amazing."

Gary is clearly a solid bloke who realises how lucky he is to be a professional tour golfer.

"Believe me, we all watch Tiger and try to learn from him," he says. And Gary is also an obvious believer in what Gary Player once said: "The more I practise, the luckier I get."

Above: Another approach shot from the middle of the fairway. And who says he doesn't hit the ball a long way.

Left: Gary Orr's two under par round took the honours at Burhill.

No hard feelings. The best man on the day took the honours.

Nick Dougherty

He's bright, he's good-looking, he's a party-animal, and he thinks
he is going to be the world number one – like Tiger.

Player stats

Age: 20.

Home: Chorley, Lancashire.

Amateur record: Won his first tournament (an under-14 event) at the age of six, and in all won international events on no less than four different continents, including the Faldo Junior Series (three years in a row), the European under-21 Championship and the World Boys Championship. He also represented England 74 times and played in the Walker Cup in 2001.

Turned pro: 2001.

Pro career: Rookie of the Year last year after finishing 36th in the Order of Merit. Had three top 10 finishes last year, including a second place at the Qatar Masters.

World Ranking March 2002: 217.

World Ranking March 2003: 194.

LOOKING BACK at this 20-year-old Lancastrian's debut year on the European Tour, his report would read something like: 'Good work, but could do better'. Indeed his 'schoolmaster' (well, okay, his Walker Cup captain) Peter McEvoy said as much. "I thought last year he should have won a tournament, and so in my view his year was one of underachievement. But, you've got to remember it was his first year out in the big bright world, and a bit like your first year at university, there are a lot of distractions out there. Of all the guys I've seen – and I've seen Donald, Casey, and Rose – Dougherty is the most exciting young player I've come across. He's got a bit of the Seve or the Sergio in him. I think he is good enough to sit back, not put in too much effort, and still be a Ryder Cup player."

Far from feeling chastised, Dougherty turns McEvoy's remarks into a positive. "It's true, I probably did party too much last year and probably at the wrong times. But I was 19 then and I think I'm more mature now. And think about it. If I was Rookie of the Year without working as hard as I should have, then presumably I could have done much better."

At the end of last year, Dougherty sat down with his dad, and his coach Pete Cowen, and they decided that one of his main goals for this year should be to take a much more professional approach to everything. "I still want to go to parties and have a good time but in the position I'm in – competing against the very best in the world – I can't afford to do what a normal 20-year-old would do."

His reputation for 'having a good time' has got him the nickname Georgie on Tour, after George Best. "It could be much worse. Some guys have names I couldn't possibly repeat," he says. In honour of his heroes (he is fanatical about Manchester United) or perhaps because "it just seemed like a good thing at the time" he has recently put red streaks in his spikey gelled hair. Trendy designer labels – like Tag Heuer and Hugo Boss – have rushed to sponsor him. And there is a queue of girls waiting to swoon in his path if his girlfriend (wannabe actress Emily Jane-Lovitt) ever decides to move aside. "We call her Bob," he says, "because she's a bit of a Tom Boy."

There is a mischievous side to Dougherty, which makes him an extrovert and an entertainer, unlikely to take anything (other than his golf) too seriously. When he goes out to dinner with Nick Faldo (which he does more often than most of us) he has been known to pretend to unwitting waitresses that he is dining with Faldo's lookalike, Harrison Ford. When his pal Luke Donald won in his first year on the US Tour, Dougherty rang him on his mobile and pulled his leg mercilessly, saying he wouldn't have won if it hadn't been a rain-shortened event.

There is another distinguishing feature about this boy who will become a man (well, 21 anyway) on May 24th. He is a very clever individual with a hugely impressive list of academic qualifications considering much of his youth was spent whacking little white balls into little white holes. He comes from a bright family; his dad is a very successful businessman, while his brother is a corporate lawyer in New York.

When he's not playing golf, Dougherty is learning to fly and hopes some day to get his pilot's license. He also plays the flute. "My dad was a huge Beatles fan and he used to own one of Paul McCartney's first guitars. But he traded this in to buy a flute for me when I was at primary school." Dougherty's intelligence will ensure he doesn't fritter away his talent by overselling his very marketable image in an Anna Kournikova sort of way.

"I'm a much better player than I was a year ago," he says. "My consistency has improved immeasurably, because 12 months ago when I hit a bad shot it was really bad. That's changed now. That's the great thing about Tiger, he can play badly and still shoot 70, and I am getting nearer to that point."

Dougherty still recognises that Tiger Woods is some way ahead of him in the pecking order, not least in experience and pure physical strength. But he is working harder to try to close that gap.

"Tiger is beatable if you take the right attitude onto the course while playing him. He is only a guy playing golf. He makes mistakes – not many – but he makes them. I've studied him a lot. If there's one thing he's taught me it's his approach on the course. His aggression when he is playing is extraordinary. I'm working on trying to establish a competitive fire like that, which can best be described as 'cold fury'.

Can you be World No.1?
If I can just continue what I am doing I'm sure I will be. I wouldn't be at all intimidated playing Tiger tomorrow. It's weird but I tend to raise my game when it matters.

PHOTOGRAPHY: PHIL SHELDON

INTERVIEW: JOCK HOWARD

"Tiger is beatable if you take the right attitude onto the course while playing him."

Paul Casey

This Englishman living in Arizona is about to burst onto the world stage, and he can outdrive Tiger with something to spare.

Player stats

Age: 25.

Home: Phoenix, Arizona.

Amateur record: Won the prestigious American college event the Pac-10 Champs three years in a row, 1998-2000, English Amateur Championship 1999, Walker Cup 1999, English Amateur Championship 2000, ASU Thunderbird Invitational 2000.

Turned pro: 2000.

Pro career: Finished joint 12th in his first pro start in a European Tour event at the 2001 Benson & Hedges and soon after gained his first victory at the 2001 Scottish PGA Championship, which gained him the Rookie of the Year award. In 2002 he had four top 10 finishes and finished 46th on the Order of Merit, before winning his second pro event at the ANZ Championship in Australia earlier this year.

World Ranking March 2002: 97.

World Ranking March 2003: 60.

A 10-year-old boy is watching the Masters on television at home in Walton-on-Thames. His dad sits beside him, shouting at Sandy Lyle's ball, as it teeters on the top tier of the 18th green. As the ball begins to roll down towards the hole, father is out of his chair, blowing it back down the green. The ball eventually comes to rest eight feet from the hole, and the rest (Sandy's jig and the hug with his caddie Dave Musgrove) is history.

From that moment on, the 10-year-old wanted to be a pro golfer. The big question was whether he would be talented enough, although that is not a question which has ever troubled the boy himself. Ask him now, 15 years later, to describe when he realised he was good enough to achieve his dream and he will look at you blankly.

"I always thought I was good enough, even when I was a beginner. It wasn't a case of there being a defining moment, or the light suddenly switching on. People who do well always believe they are going to do well. I guess maybe I must possess some sort of inner arrogance but it was never something I doubted," he says.

You might think that as well as a wonderfully powerful swing, Casey possesses a staggeringly swollen ego. But you would be wrong. In just two years as a professional he has already shown enough signs that he is on his way to the top, and his two wins (one earlier this year in Australia) have underlined his natural ability.

The ease with which he has gone from being a very successful amateur (he is one of only three GB&I players in 80 years of Walker Cup history to win four matches and lose none) to a very good professional has been seamless. His confidence in his own ability is shared by five members at his club, Burhill in Surrey. When he turned professional, they put a bet on him to win a major within five years. If it happens they stand to pick up a six-figure sum.

"I've learnt a lot from Ian Poulter," says Casey. "He could walk on to a stage with a microphone and think he was the best singer in the world, if that's what he wanted to do. That's an amazing ability because you are able to believe that you belong even if you don't."

The first thing you notice about Paul Casey is his physical strength. Much of the skill in the golf swing comes from the forearms, and the spinach-eating Popeye would be proud of this guy's forearms. Casey also doesn't get frightened when he shoots low scores. He is a streaky player, capable of shooting really low numbers, but when he gets to 7 or 8 under par he doesn't panic and go backwards.

He also doesn't seem to have that mental block when it comes to dealing with that man called Eldrick which so many players from the generation above him do. Unlike Mickelson, Montgomerie, Duval and even Ernie, Casey hasn't spent the past seven years being hammered into the ground.

"A lot of people assume I and a few of

the other young players were inspired to start by Tiger," says Casey, "but he's only two years older than me. Seve, Langer, Faldo, Woosie and Lyle were the ones who inspired me when they were winning the Open and the Masters. I think guys my age might be a little bit fresher. We don't have that shadow hanging over our heads. We probably look at him a bit differently and we think we can learn from what he's done and then go out and beat him. Players who were at the top of the game before Tiger, looking as though they could be the best in the world, and have now been displaced by him, must find it incredibly difficult mentally. We don't have so many negative experiences."

Casey played eight holes with Tiger (and Adam Scott) in a practice round before the WGC World Match Play Championship, back in February. "If there is one thing which impresses me about him more than anything else is that he can win an event – say by 20 shots – then sit down at home on Sunday night and still ask himself what he did wrong. Then, he'll go out and work on it. That's the key. He knows he doesn't know it all. He has this drive to get better."

When Sam Torrance picked his team for the 2001 Ryder Cup, Casey's name was mentioned in dispatches as being incredibly close to getting in the side. "Sam's words certainly stirred something inside me. My biggest immediate goal is to be in the 2004 Ryder Cup side. Winning at team golf is an awesome experience and is a lot more fun than winning as an individual. I think that is readily available right now." It will be fascinating to see just how close he gets.

Can you be World No.1?

It may take 10 years but I think, by working hard, I am capable of that. I have the potential.

PHOTOGRAPHY: GETTY IMAGES

INTERVIEW: JOCK HOWARD

"I guess maybe I possess some sort of inner arrogance."

PUNCH YOUR WEIGHT

PAUL CASEY is one of the most exciting of the new breed of golfers to emerge recently. Not just because he's already won a couple of European Tour events, which is impressive in itself, but the way he does it. He's an aggressive golfer by nature and a real powerhouse. Not big, but strong nevertheless. One of the best things about his swing is the way he marries his arm swing with his body action; the holy grail of the golf swing. It's a very compact, tidy action and it helps him make really solid contact. As a result, Casey more than punches his weight.

What you can learn...

Control your downswing

■ Controlling what you do in the downswing is never easy, because everything is happening pretty fast, so the trick is this. Learn to co-ordinate the movement of your arm swing and body turn in your backswing and, as a result of that, your downswing will be better co-ordinated, too. The hands and arms have further to travel than the shoulders, so it makes sense they should get a head start. That's the specific 'feeling' you need. From halfway back, you should then think of the arms and body completing the backswing at the same time. These swing thoughts should help synchronise your arms and body and get you into a good slot at the top. From there, you've got a better chance of making a good downswing.

From halfway back, think about the arms and body completing the backswing at the same time.

PHOTO: GETTY IMAGES